Rock Island Public Library
401 - 19th Street
Rock Island, IL 61201-8143

D1441017

683.88 Eml   JUN   1994 ✕

Emley, Douglas.   Inv

Clothes dryer repair under
$40

No Headache Guide to Home Repair

Clothes Dryer Repair

DATE DUE

JUL 18		
AUG 9		
JAN 0 4		
	JUL 0 9 2003	
MAY 01		
AUG 1	OCT 0 8 2003	
AUG 22		
NOV 07	SEP 1 7 2003	
JAN 0 8 1997		
JUN 25		
FEB 1 6 2000		
DEC 1 0 2002		

HIGHSMITH #45115

New Century Publishing
P.O. Box 9861
Fountain Valley, CA 92708

The Author, the publisher and all interested parties have used all possible care to assure that the information contained in this book is as complete and as accurate as possible. However, neither the publisher nor the author nor any interested party assumes any liability for omissions, errors, or defects in the materials, instructions or diagrams contained in this publication, and therefore are not liable for any damages including (but not limited to) personal injury, property damage or legal disputes that may result from the use of this book.

All major appliances are complex electro-mechanical devices. Personal injury or property damage may occur before, during, or after any attempt to repair an appliance. This publication is intended for individuals posessing an adequate background of technical experience. The above named parties are not responsible for an individual's judgement of his or her own technical abilities and experience, and therefore are not liable for any damages including (but not limited to) personal injury, property damage or legal disputes that may result from such judgements.

The advice and opinions offered by this publication are of a subjective nature ONLY and they are NOT to be construed as legal advice. The above named parties are not responsible for the interpretation or implementation of subjective advice and opinions, and therefore are not responsible for any damages including (but not limited to) personal injury, property damage, or legal disputes that may result from such interpretation or implementation.

The use of this publication acknowledges the understanding and acceptance of the above terms and conditions.

Acknowledgment

The author and the publisher wish to thank technical consultant, Dick Miller, for his expert advice and assistance in the compilation of technical information and procedure contained in this publication.

©1994 Douglas Emley

Publishcd by New Century Publishing
P.O. Box 9861
Fountain Valley, CA 92708

All rights reserved. No portion of this book may be copied or reprinted without the express prior written permission of New Century Publishing, with the exception of a review of this book whereby brief passages may be quoted by the reviewer with proper credit line. Write for permission to the above address.

International Standard Book Number   1-884348-01-7

Printed in the United States of America

Table Of Contents

FOREWORD

WHAT THIS BOOK WILL DO FOR YOU
(and what it won't!)

This book **will** tell you how to fix the most common problems with the most common brands of domestic (household) dryers. (This represents 95+ percent of all repairs that the average handyman or service tech will run into.)

This book **will not** tell you how to fix your industrial or commercial or any very large dryer. The support and control systems for such units are usually very similar in function to those of smaller units, but vastly different in design, service and repair.

We **will** show you the easiest and/or fastest method of diagnosing and repairing your dryer.

We **will not necessarily** show you the absolute cheapest way of doing something. Sometimes, when the cost of a part is just a few dollars, we advocate replacing the part rather than rebuilding it. We also sometimes advocate replacement of an inexpensive part, whether it's good or bad, as a simplified method of diagnosis or as a preventive measure.

We **will** use only the simplest of tools; tools that a well-equipped home mechanic is likely to have and to know how to use, including a VOM.

We **will not** advocate your buying several hundred dollars' worth of exotic equipment or special tools, or getting advanced technical training to make a one-time repair. It will usually cost you less to have a professional perform this type of repair. Such repairs represent only a very small percentage of all needed repairs.

We **do not** discuss electrical or mechanical theories. There are already many very well-written textbooks on these subjects and most of them are not likely to be pertinent to the job at hand; fixing your dryer!

We **do** discuss rudimentary mechanical systems and simple electrical circuits.

We expect you to be able to look at a part and remove it if the mounting bolts and/or connections are obvious. If the mounting mechanism is complicated or hidden, or there are tricks to removing or installing something, we'll tell you about it.

You are expected to know what certain electrical and mechanical devices are, what they do in general, and how they work. For example, switches, relays, heater elements, motors, solenoids, cams, pullies, idlers, belts, radial and thrust (axial) bearings, flexible motor couplings, splines, gas valves, air seals, and centrifugal blowers and axial-flow fans. If you do not know what these things do, learn them BEFORE you start working on your dryer.

You should know how to cut, strip, and splice wire with crimp-on connectors, wire nuts and electrical tape. You should know how to measure voltage and how to test for continuity with a VOM (Volt-Ohm Meter). If you have an ammeter, you should know how and where to measure the current in amps. If you don't know how to use these meters, there's a brief course on how to use them (for *our* purposes *only*) in Chapter 1. See section 1-4 before you buy either or both of these meters.

A given procedure was only included in this book if it passed the following criteria:
1) The job is something that the average couch potato can complete in one afternoon, with no prior knowledge of the machine, with tools a normal home handyman is likely to have.
2) The parts and/or special tools required to complete the job are easily found and not too expensive.
3) The problem is a common one; occuring more frequently than just one out of a hundred machines.

Certain repairs which may cost more than $30 may be included in this book, if they pass the following criteria:
1) The cost of the repair is still far less than replacing the machine or calling a professional service technician, and
2) The repair is likely to yield a machine that will operate satisfactorily for several more years, or at least long enough to justify the cost.

In certain parts of the book, the author expresses an opinion as to whether the current value of a particular machine warrants making the repair or ''scrapping'' the machine. Such opinions are to be construed as opinions ONLY and they are NOT to be construed as legal advice. The decision as to whether to take a particular machine out of service depends on a number of factors that the author cannot possibly know and has no control over; therefore, the responsibility for such a decision rests solely with the person making the decision.

I'm sure that a physicist reading this book could have a lot of fun tearing it apart because of my deliberate avoidance and misuse of technical terms. However, this manual is written to simplify the material and inform the novice, not to appease the scientist.

*NOTE: The diagnosis and repair procedures in this manual do not necessarily apply to brand-new units, newly-installed units or recently relocated units. Although they **may** posess the problems described in this manual, dryers that have recently been installed or moved are subject to special considerations not taken into account in this manual for the sake of simplicity. Such special considerations include installation parameters, installation location, the possibility of manufacturing or construction defects, damage in transit, and others.*

This manual was designed to assist the novice technician in the repair of home (domestic) dryers that have been operating successfully for an extended period of months or years and have only recently stopped operating properly, with no major change in installation parameters or location.

HOW TO USE THIS BOOK

STEP 1: PLEASE READ THE DISCLAIMER LOCATED ON THE COPYRIGHT PAGE. This book is intended for use by people who have a little bit of mechanical experience or aptitude, and just need a little coaching when it comes to appliances. If you don't fit that category, you may want to rethink trying to fix it yourself! We're all bloomin' lawyers these days, y'know? If you break something or hurt yourself, no one is responsible but **you**; not the author, the publisher, the guy or the store who sold you this book, or anyone else. If you don't understand the disclaimer, get a lawyer to translate it **before** you start working.

Read the safety and repair precautions in section 1-5. These should help you avoid making any *really* bad mistakes.

STEP 2: READ CHAPTERS 1 & 2: Everything else in this book flows from chapters 1 and 2. *If you don't read them, you won't be able to properly diagnose your dryer.*

Know what kind of dryer you have and basically how it works. When you go to the appliance parts dealer, have the nameplate information at hand. Have the proper tools at hand, and know how to use them.

STEP 3: READ THE CHAPTER ABOUT YOUR SPECIFIC BRAND AND MODEL.

STEP 4: FIX THE BLOOMIN' THING! If you can, of course. If you're just too confused, or if the book recommends calling a technician for a complex operation, call one.

Chapter 1

DRYER IDENTIFICATION
TOOLS & SAFETY
TIPS & TRICKS

1-1. BRAND IDENTIFICATION

Appliance companies, like most other major industries, have their share of take-overs, buyouts and cross-brand agreements.

Besides the six primary dryer brands listed in this book, the following brands are covered. In some cases, the dryers were manufactured by the same companies under a different brand name. In other cases, the companies merged, or one bought the other.

ADMIRAL: Norge

AMANA: Speed Queen

ESTATE: Whirlpool

FRANKLIN: WCI

FRIGIDAIRE: Since the late 70's, Frigidaire has been manufactured by WCI. Recently, WCI changed their name back to the Frigidaire Company.

GIBSON: WCI

JC PENNEY: General Electric

HOTPOINT: General Electric

KELVINATOR: WCI

KENMORE: Whirlpool

KITCHENAID: Whirlpool

MAGIC CHEF: Norge

MONTGOMERY WARD: For a long time, Norge. More recently, WCI.

PENNCREST: General Electric

ROPER: Whirlpool

SIGNATURE: Norge or WCI

WHITE-WESTINGHOUSE: WCI

1-2 BEFORE YOU START

Find yourself a good appliance parts dealer. You can find them in the yellow pages under the following headings:

● APPLIANCES, HOUSEHOLD, MAJOR
● APPLIANCES, PARTS AND SUPPLIES
● REFRIGERATORS, DOMESTIC
● APPLIANCES, HOUSEHOLD, REPAIR AND SERVICE

Call a few of them and ask if they are a repair service, or if they sell parts, or both. Ask them if they offer free advice with the parts they sell. (Occasionally, stores that offer both parts and service will not want to give you advice.) Often the parts counter men are ex-technicians who got tired of the pressures of in-home service. They can be your best friends. However, you don't want to badger them with TOO many questions, so know your basics before you start asking questions.

Some parts houses may offer service, too. Be careful! There may be a conflict of interest. They may try to talk you out of even trying to fix your own dryer. They'll tell you it's too complicated, then in the same breath ''guide'' you to their service department. Who are you gonna believe, me or them? Not all service and parts places are this way, however. If they genuinely try to help you fix it yourself, and you find that you're unable to, they may be the best place to look for service.

When you go into the store, have ready the make, model and serial number from the nameplate of the dryer.

NAMEPLATE INFORMATION

The metal nameplate is usually found in one of the places shown in figure B-1:

A) Along the bottom panel, on the left or right corner.

B) Inside the door.

C) Somewhere on the back of the dryer.

D) On the side or top of the console.

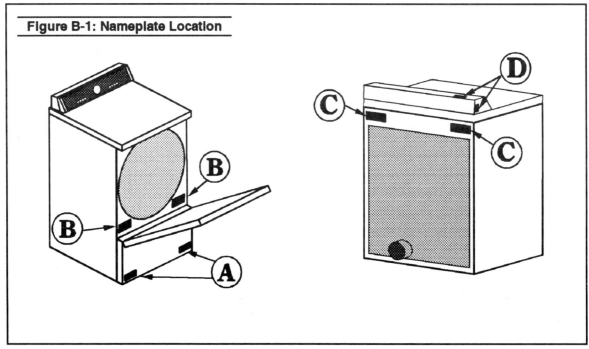

Figure B-1: Nameplate Location

If all else fails, check the original papers that came with your dryer when it was new. They should contain the model number somewhere.

In any case, and especially if you have absolutely NO information about your dryer anywhere, make sure you bring your old part to the parts store with you. Sometimes they can match it up by looks or by part number.

1-3 TOOLS (Figure B-2)

The tools that you may need (depending on the diagnosis) are listed below. Some are optional. The reason for the option is explained.

For certain repairs, you will need a special tool. These are inexpensively available from your appliance parts dealer. They are listed in this book as needed.

SCREWDRIVERS: Both flat and phillips head; two or three sizes of each. It's best to have at least a stubby, 4- and 6-inch sizes.

NUTDRIVERS: You will need at least 1/4" and 5/16" sizes. 4- or 6-inch ones should suffice, but it's better to have a stubby, too. A certain procedure when working on gas valves (Chapter 2, replacing the split coil assembly) requires a 7/32" nutdriver in most cases.

ELECTRICAL PLIERS or STRIPPERS and DIAGONAL CUTTING PLIERS: For cutting and stripping small electrical wire.

ALLIGATOR JUMPERS (sometimes called a "CHEATER" or "CHEATER WIRE":) Small guage (14-16 guage or so) and about 12-18 inches long, for testing electrical circuits. Available at your local electronics store. Cost: a few bucks for 4 or 5 of them.

BUTT CONNECTORS, CRIMPERS, WIRE NUTS and ELECTRICAL TAPE: For splicing small wire.

VOM (VOLT-OHM METER) For testing electrical circuits. If you do not have one, get one. An inexpensive one will suffice, as long as it has both "AC Voltage" and "Resistance" (i.e. Rx1, Rx10) settings on the dial. It will do for our purposes.

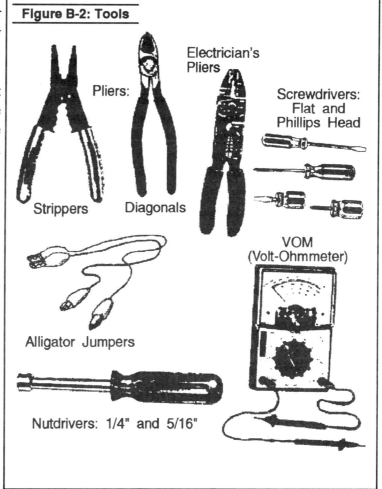

Figure B-2: Tools

Pliers:

Electrician's Pliers

Screwdrivers: Flat and Phillips Head

Strippers   Diagonals

VOM (Volt-Ohmmeter)

Alligator Jumpers

Nutdrivers: 1/4" and 5/16"

OPTIONAL TOOLS (Figure B-3)

SNAP-AROUND AMMETER: For determining if electrical components are energized. Quite useful; but a bit expensive, and there are alternate methods. If you have one, use it; otherwise, don't bother getting one.

EXTENDABLE INSPECTION MIRROR: For seeing difficult places beneath the dryer and behind panels.

CORDLESS POWER SCREWDRIVER OR DRILL/DRIVER WITH MAGNETIC SCREWDRIVER AND NUTDRIVER TIPS: For pulling off panels held in place by many screws. It can save you lots of time and hassle.

1-4. HOW TO USE A VOM AND AMMETER

Many home handymen are very intimidated by electricity. It's true that diagnosing and repairing electrical circuits requires a *bit* more care than most operations, due to the danger of getting shocked. But there is no mystery or voodoo about the things we'll be doing. Remember the rule in section 1-5 (1); while you are working on a circuit, energize the circuit only long enough to perform whatever test you're performing, then take the power back off it to perform the repair. You need not be concerned with any theory, like what an ohm is, or what a volt is. You will only need to be able to set the VOM onto the right scale, touch the test leads to the right place and read the meter.

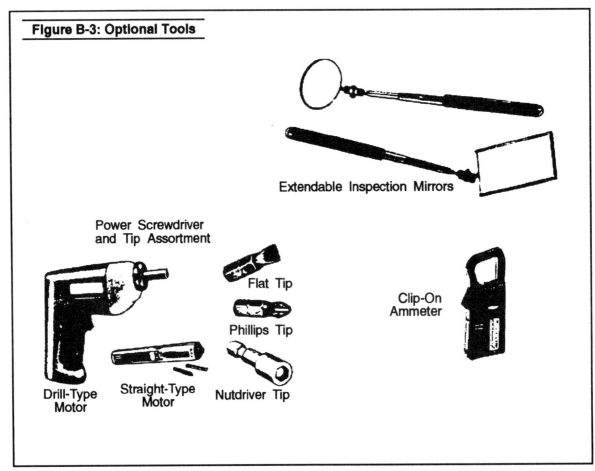

Figure B-3: Optional Tools

Extendable Inspection Mirrors

Power Screwdriver and Tip Assortment

Flat Tip

Phillips Tip

Clip-On Ammeter

Drill-Type Motor

Straight-Type Motor

Nutdriver Tip

In using the VOM (Volt-Ohm Meter) for our purposes, the two test leads are always plugged into the "+" and "-" holes on the VOM. (Some VOMs have more than two holes.)

1-4(a). TESTING VOLTAGE (Figure B-4)

Set the dial of the VOM on the lowest VAC scale (A.C. Voltage) over 120 volts. For example, if there's a 50 setting and a 250 setting on the VAC dial, use the 250 scale, because 250 is the lowest setting over 120 volts.

Touch the two test leads to the two metal contacts of a live power source, like a wall outlet or the terminals of the motor that you're testing for voltage. (*Do not* **jam** *the test leads into a wall outlet!*) If you are getting power through the VOM, the meter will jump up and steady on a reading. You *may* have to convert the scale in your head. For example, if you're using the 250 volt dial setting and the meter has a "25" scale, simply divide by 10; 120 volts would be "12" on the meter.

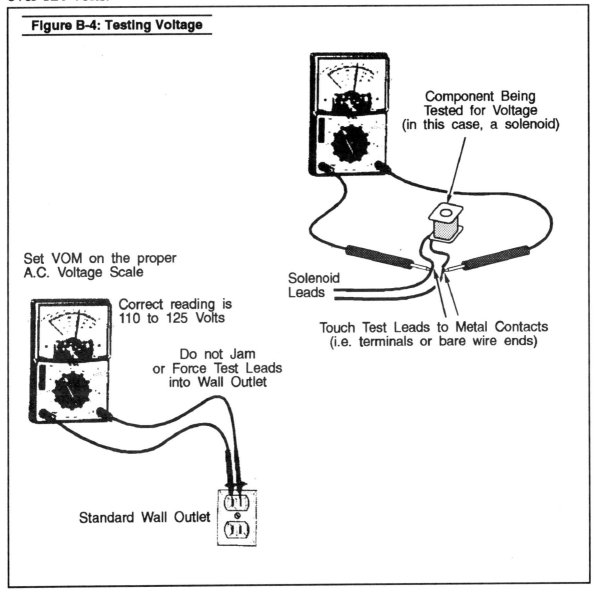

Figure B-4: Testing Voltage

Set VOM on the proper A.C. Voltage Scale

Correct reading is 110 to 125 Volts

Do not Jam or Force Test Leads into Wall Outlet

Standard Wall Outlet

Component Being Tested for Voltage (in this case, a solenoid)

Solenoid Leads

Touch Test Leads to Metal Contacts (i.e. terminals or bare wire ends)

1-4(b). TESTING FOR CONTINUITY (Figure B-5)

Don't let the word "continuity" scare you. It's derived from the word "continuous." In an electrical circuit, electricity has to flow *from* a power source back *to* that power source. If there is any break in the circuit, it is not continuous, and it has no continuity. "Good" continuity means that there is no break in the circuit.

For example, if you were testing a solenoid to see if it was burned out, you would try putting a small amount of power through the solenoid. If it was burned out, there would be a break in the circuit, the electricity wouldn't flow, and your meter would show no continuity.

That is what the resistance part of your VOM does; it provides a small electrical current (using batteries within the VOM) and measures how fast the current is flowing. For our purposes, it doesn't matter how *fast* the current is flowing; only that there *is* current flow.

To use your VOM to test continuity, set the dial on (resistance) R x 1, or whatever the lowest setting is. Touch the metal parts of the test leads together and read the meter. It should peg the meter all the way on the right side of the scale, towards "0" on the meter's "resistance" scale. If the meter does not read zero resistance, adjust the thumbwheel on the front of the VOM until it *does* read zero. If you cannot get the meter to read zero, the battery in the VOM is low; replace it.

If you are testing, say, a solenoid, first make sure that the solenoid leads are not connected to anything, especially a power source. If the solenoid's leads are still connected to something, you may get a reading through that something. If there is still live power on the item you're testing

for continuity, you will burn out your VOM instantly and possibly shock yourself.

Touch the two test leads to the two bare wire ends or terminals of the solenoid. You can touch the ends of the wires and

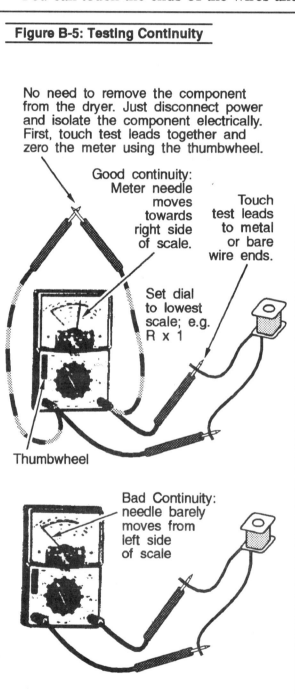

Figure B-5: Testing Continuity

No need to remove the component from the dryer. Just disconnect power and isolate the component electrically. First, touch test leads together and zero the meter using the thumbwheel.

Good continuity: Meter needle moves towards right side of scale.

Touch test leads to metal or bare wire ends.

Set dial to lowest scale; e.g. R x 1

Thumbwheel

Bad Continuity: needle barely moves from left side of scale

test leads with your hands if necessary to get better contact. The voltage that the VOM batteries put out is very low, and you will not be shocked. If there is NO continuity, the meter won't move. If there is GOOD continuity, the meter will move toward the right side of the scale and steady on a reading. This is the resistance reading and it doesn't concern us; we only care that we show good continuity. If the meter moves only very little and stays towards the left side of the scale, that's BAD continuity; the solenoid is no good.

If you are testing a switch, you will show little or no resistance (good continuity) when the switch is closed, and NO continuity when the switch is open. If you do not, the switch is bad.

1-4(c). AMMETERS

Ammeters are a little bit more complex to explain without going into a lot of electrical theory. If you own an ammeter, you probably already know how to use it.

If you don't, don't get one. Ammeters are expensive. And for *our* purposes, there are other ways to determine what an ammeter tests for. If you don't own one, skip this section.

For our purposes, ammeters are simply a way of testing for continuity without having to cut into the system or to disconnect power from whatever it is we're testing.

Ammeters measure the current in amps flowing through a wire. The greater the current that's flowing *through* a wire, the greater the density of the magnetic field, or *flux*, it produces *around* the wire. The ammeter simply measures the density of this flux, and thus the amount of current, flowing through the wire. To determine continuity, for our purposes, we can simply isolate the component that we're testing (so we do not accidentally measure the current going through any other components) and see if there's *any* current flow.

To use your ammeter, first make sure that it's on an appropriate scale (0 to 10 or 20 amps will do). Isolate a wire leading directly to the component you're testing. Put the ammeter loop around that wire and read the meter. (Figure B-6)

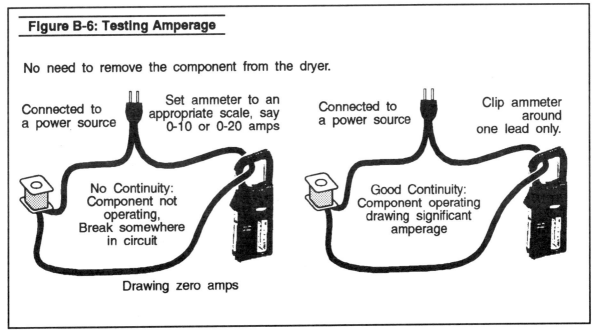

Figure B-6: Testing Amperage

No need to remove the component from the dryer.

Connected to a power source

Set ammeter to an appropriate scale, say 0-10 or 0-20 amps

No Continuity: Component not operating, Break somewhere in circuit

Drawing zero amps

Connected to a power source

Clip ammeter around one lead only.

Good Continuity: Component operating drawing significant amperage

1-5. BASIC REPAIR AND SAFETY PRECAUTIONS

1) Always de-energize (pull the plug or trip the breaker on) any dryer that you're disassembling. If you need to re-energize the dryer to perform a test, make sure any bare wires or terminals are taped or insulated. Energize the unit only long enough to perform whatever test you're performing, then disconnect the power again.

2) If the manual advocates replacing the part, REPLACE IT!! You might find, say, a solenoid that has jammed for no apparent reason. Sometimes you can clean it out and lubricate it, and get it going again. The key words here are *apparent reason*. There is a reason that it stopped. You can bet on it. And if you get it going and re-install it, you are running a very high risk that it will stop again. If *that* happens, you will have to start repairing your dryer *all* over again. It may only act up when it is hot, or it may be bent slightly...there are a hundred different ''what if's.'' Very few of the parts mentioned in this book will cost you over ten or twenty dollars. Replace the part.

3) If you must lay the dryer over on its side, front or back, first make sure that you are not going to break anything off, such as a gas valve. Lay an old blanket on the floor to protect the floor and the finish of the dryer.

4) Always replace the green (ground) leads when you remove an electrical component. They're there for a reason. And NEVER EVER remove the third (ground) prong in the main power plug!

5) When opening the dryer cabinet or console, remember that the sheet metal parts are have very sharp edges. Wear gloves, and be careful not to cut your hands!

6) When testing for your power supply from a wall outlet, plug in a small appliance such as a shaver or blow dryer. If you're not getting full power out of the outlet, you'll know it right away.

7) If you have diagnosed a certain part to be bad, but you cannot figure out how to remove it, sometimes it helps to get the new part and examine it for mounting holes or other clues as to how it may be mounted.

Chapter 2

DRYER BASICS
TROUBLESHOOTING
REPAIRS COMMON TO ALL BRANDS

2-1 DRYER BASICS & COMPONENTS

The main idea of a dryer is to circulate warm air through wet clothes to evaporate moisture from them. This sounds really simple, but there are many implications. This means that all dryers have to have a blower to move air and a heat source to warm the air, and that airflow is very important. It also means that all dryers must have a way to toss the clothes around a bit, because air won't circulate through them if they're just laying there in a big wet lump. This is done by "tumbling" them in a big round drum.

The main differences between different makes and models are the way the drum is supported, the layout of any electric heaters, and airflow.

2-1(a) DRIVE TRAIN (Figure G-1)

All dryers have a drive motor which turns the drum through a belt. In most dryers, the motor also turns a blower fan connected directly to the motor shaft; in a few notable exceptions, the fan is belted off the drive motor, too.

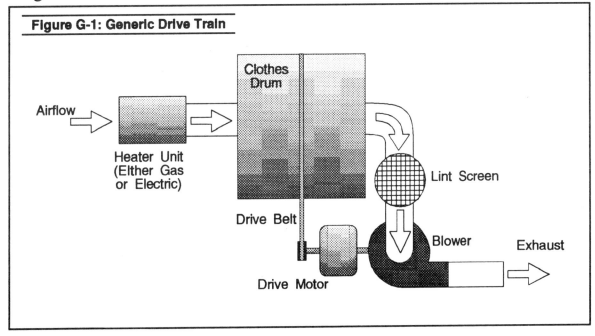

Figure G-1: Generic Drive Train

Airflow — Heater Unit (Either Gas or Electric) — Clothes Drum — Drive Belt — Drive Motor — Lint Screen — Blower — Exhaust

2-1(b) HEAT SOURCE AND TEMPERATURE CONTROL

Warm air evaporates moisture much faster than cold air, so all dryers also have a heat source. The heat source in household machines is either gas or electric. Electric heating elements come in many different configurations; see the chapter about your brand for details. Gas burners are remarkably similar in all the different brands. Ignitor systems and holding coils on the gas safety valves have varied slightly over the years, but you can find the diagnosis and repair procedures for all gas burners covered by this manual in section 2-3.

A temperature control system keeps the air at the optimum temperature for drying and prevents scorching of your clothes. This system uses several thermostats; some adjustable and others a fixed temperature. Testing the temperature control system is discussed in section 2-4(c). Finding the thermostats is discussed in the chapter pertaining to your model.

There is also a safety system that prevents the heating system from starting at all unless the blower is turning. This prevents overheating of the system or natural gas buildup in the dryer cabinet. A contact in the centrifugal motor starting switch assembly only allows the heating system to heat if the motor is running.

2-1(c) AIRFLOW, LINT FILTER AND EXHAUST SYSTEM

Airflow is important in removing the moisture from the dryer drum; thus the blower, vents and exhaust ducting must be kept as clean (translation: free of lint) as possible. This also prevents overheating of electric heating elements and accidental lint fires, and insures enough airflow to keep the gas burner operating properly.

Also, drum seals can wear out and leak, which can disrupt proper airflow.

The lint screen traps most lint, but some does get through or leak out around the drum seals. Over a period of years enough can build up enough to allow some of the above symptoms to occur. The airflow system is discussed in section 2-5, except for drum seals, which are discussed in the chapter pertaining to your brand of dryer.

In most models, the blower is the last component in the airflow system. (See Figure G-1) From the blower, the air goes directly out the dryer exhaust. Thus, the other components are *not* under *pressure*. Air is being *sucked* through them, so they are under a *vacuum*.

2-1(d) TIMERS AND OTHER CONTROLS

Some dryer timers are simply devices that run the motor for a set number of minutes; others integrate temperature control and even moisture (humidity) controls. Yet others are solid-state, electronic units. If you have a separate timer and temperature control, consider yourself lucky; the combined units are considerably more difficult to diagnose and generally more expensive to replace. Diagnosis is discussed in Chapter 2-4(b).

2-2 SYMPTOMS

Dryers are relatively simple machines; they just don't have many components. So most repairs stem from just a few common complaints:

1) NOISY OPERATION

A vast majority of these complaints stem from drum supports that have worn out. It usually sounds like a loud, low-pitched rumbling sound that slowly gets worse over a period of several months or even years. This is a very common complaint in Whirlpool or Kenmore brand dryers about 7 to 15 years old. See the chapter about your brand for specifics about replacing the drum support rollers.

In some models, notably GE, if a belt breaks, the drum tensioner will touch the drive motor shaft and a loud grinding or clattering noise will result. Replace the belt as described in the chapter about your brand.

You may get a rumbling noise if a belt tensioner pulley seizes up or the tensioner spring breaks.

A regular clack-clack sound as the dryer drum is turning may be coins stuck inside the removable plastic dryer vanes. This can happen in Whirlpool or Kenmore dryers, as well as some other brands, though it is infrequent. To solve the problem, open the top of ther dryer as described in the Whirlpool section, then remove the plastic vane on the inside of the dryer drum by removing the screws on the outside of the dryer drum that hold it in place.

In some models, notably Maytag and Frigidaire machines, things can get by the lint screen (like pencils and pens) and get stuck in the blower wheel. Again, it's a loud grinding sound, as if you were sticking something into a moving blower fan. See the section about your brand for details about how to get to the blower in your machine.

2) NOT DRYING WELL
(See also NO HEAT below)

Usually this is caused by poor airflow. Feel the dryer vent exhaust (usually outside the house.) If there isn't a strong blast of air coming out, check the lint screen and open up any dryer vent you can get to to check for clogging. Also check any flexible dryer vent for pinching.

In some machines, if the drum is not turning, there will be no noise or other external symptoms. The clothes will simply be laying there in a big wet lump and they won't dry. The dryer probably won't *sound* normal either. To diagnose, start the machine empty, open the door and look inside quickly, or depress the door switch to see if the drum is turning. If not, the belt or belt tensioner may be broken. To repair, see the chapter about your brand.

You may see similar symptoms if the motor has gone bad, except that you probably will not hear the motor turning. If the motor is locked, you may hear it buzzing. See section 2-4(d) about motors.

3) NO HEAT, OR LOW HEAT

This *can* be caused by poor airflow in all dryers, but *especially* in gas dryers. Check the dryer vent and exhaust as described in NOT DRYING WELL above.

This can also be caused by a problem with the air heating system within the dryer. See section 2-4(c) about thermostats and temperature control systems, section 2-3(a) about gas burners, or section 2-4(f) and the chapter about your brand for information about electric heating elements.

4) DRUM NOT TURNING
See "NOT DRYING WELL" above.

2-3 GAS BURNERS

To access the burner assembly, open the gas burner inspection door. Unless specified otherwise in the section about your dryer brand, this door is found on the lower left or right front of the dryer cabinet.

Gas burners can generally be divided into two broad categories; pilot and pilotless ignition. Pilot ignition models have not been manufactured in a number of years, and thus tend to be older units, but there are still a significant number of them in operation.

The main components of the system (see Figure G-2) are the gas valve, venturi and burner chamber, and gas safety solenoids (in all models,) the flame sensor and the ignitor (in pilotless models,) or the pilot orifice and sensor (in pilot models.)

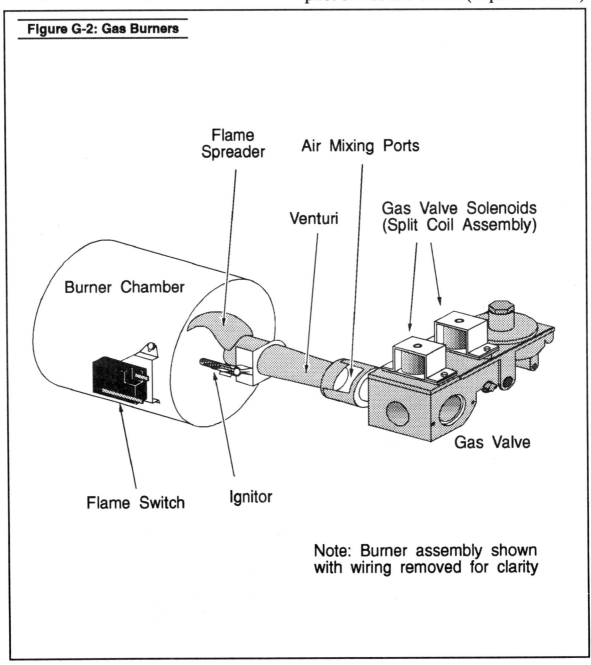

Figure G-2: Gas Burners

Flame Spreader

Air Mixing Ports

Venturi

Gas Valve Solenoids (Split Coil Assembly)

Burner Chamber

Gas Valve

Flame Switch

Ignitor

Note: Burner assembly shown with wiring removed for clarity

IGNITORS

See figure G-3 for pictures of the different types of ignitors.

Most ignitors just glow until the mechanism opens the gas valve. The ''warp switch'' ignitor sparks to ignite the gas (see ''NORMAL BURNER OPERATION'' below.) If you have a ''glo-sil'' ignitor, (it looks like a tiny coil) and it is burnt out, you are probably out of luck. They are difficult and expensive to get parts for, and considering the age of these dryers, you will probably end up getting a new dryer.

NORMAL BURNER OPERATION

A normally operating gas burner system will have a clean, mostly blue flame (perhaps occasionally streaked with just a little tinge of orange) that cycles on and off every couple of minutes.

When the flame is off and starts to cycle on, you will hear a loud click. In a pilot system, the gas valve will open and the flame will kick on at this time. In a pilotless system, the ignitor will heat up and glow brightly for about 7-15 seconds. The flame sensor senses the heat from the ignitor. If it is glowing, you will hear another click, the gas valve will open and the flame will kick on. This is a safety feature; if you don't have ignition, you certainly don't want to open the gas valve and dump gas into the dryer cabinet.

Models with a spark ignitor, or ''warp switch'' ignitor act slightly differently. Instead of the ignitor glowing, you will hear a metallic rattling sound and see what looks almost like a welder's arc flashing. The flame starts immediately and after about 15-20 seconds, the metallic rattling will stop but the flame will stay on.

When the air in the dryer drum reaches the chosen temperature (as sensed by the thermostats) the gas valve will close and the flame will shut off.

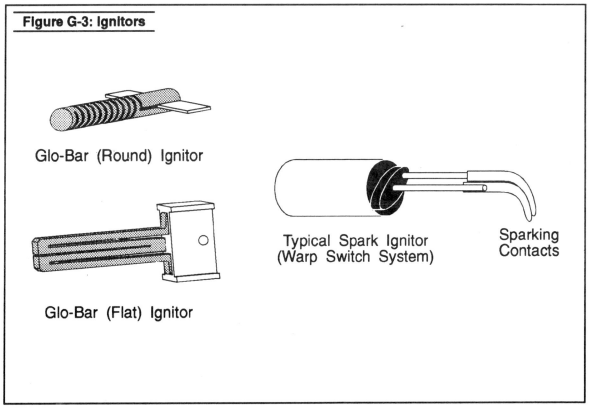

Figure G-3: Ignitors

Glo-Bar (Round) Ignitor

Glo-Bar (Flat) Ignitor

Typical Spark Ignitor
(Warp Switch System)

Sparking
Contacts

2-3(a) GAS BURNER SYMPTOMS AND REPAIR

IGNITOR DOESN'T GLOW (PILOTLESS SYSTEMS ONLY)

Nine times out of ten, if the ignitor is not glowing, it is burnt out. Unplug the dryer and remove the burner assembly as shown in figure G-4. Usually you will see a white or yellowish burned area and a break in the ignitor. If so, replace the ignitor. If you can't see an obvious break, test the ignitor for continuity as described in section 2-4(e).

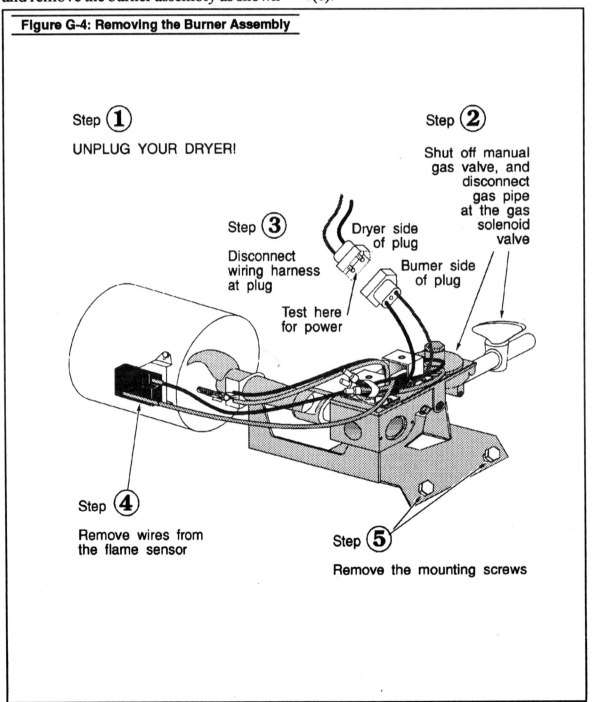

Figure G-4: Removing the Burner Assembly

Step (1)

UNPLUG YOUR DRYER!

Step (2)

Shut off manual gas valve, and disconnect gas pipe at the gas solenoid valve

Step (3)

Disconnect wiring harness at plug

Dryer side of plug

Burner side of plug

Test here for power

Step (4)

Remove wires from the flame sensor

Step (5)

Remove the mounting screws

If the ignitor is not defective , you need to isolate whether the problem is in the control (thermostat) area, or at the burner itself. The general idea is that if you have 110 volts getting to the burner assembly, then the thermostats are OK, and something in the burner assembly is bad. If you don't have 110 volts at the burner, then a thermostat or some other control is bad. Perform the following test:

1) Unplug the dryer and open the burner inspection cover as described in the chapter about your brand.

2) Unplug the main wiring harness leading to the burner assembly. (Figure G-4)

3) Using your alligator jumpers, connect a VOM to the *dryer* side of the harness plug. (as opposed to the side of the harness plug that's connected to the *burner*.)

4) Make sure no wires will get caught up in the turning drum. Set your dryer timer to the ''on'' position, high heat, and plug in the dryer. If your VOM reads 110 volts, something in the burner assembly is bad. If the burner *isn't* getting voltage, the problem is in one of the components of the heating control system: a thermostat, timer or temperature control switch, or motor centrifugal switch.

If you trace it to the burner assembly, and you've already eliminated the ignitor as the problem, either the flame sensor or the gas valve solenoid coil(s) are bad. Unplug the dryer, disconnect the flame sensor and test it for continuity. If you have no continuity, the flame sensor is bad. If you have continuity, the coils are bad. Bring the burner assembly to your parts dealer to make sure you get the right coil assembly, and don't forget to bring the model number of the machine.

SPARKER DOESN'T SPARK, OR FLAME DOESN'T START (WARP SWITCH SYSTEM ONLY)

In the older models mentioned previously, if you do not hear the metallic rattling sound, the ignitor may be out of adjustment. It can be a difficult and complex adjustment to make. Take the burner assembly to your parts dealer and they should be able to help you adjust it or guide you to someone who can.

IGNITOR GLOWS, BUT FLAME DOES NOT START (GAS VALVE DOES NOT OPEN) (PILOTLESS SYSTEMS ONLY)

Either the flame sensor is not working properly or the safety solenoid coils are not opening the gas valve. If the ignitor doesn't stop glowing, the flame sensor is bad. If the ignitor cycles on and off, the gas solenoid coil(s) are bad.

FLAME STARTS (GAS VALVE OPENS) BUT KICKS OFF QUICKLY (SHORT-CYCLES, LOW HEAT)

Usually this problem can be traced to airflow problems, especially if the flame is very orangey-colored while it is on (rather than blue.) The solution is to clean out your lint screen or dryer exhaust. It is an especially common problem in installations where the dryer exhaust runs a long way before venting to the outside. Repair as described in section 2-5.

This may also be caused by a defective flame sensor. Test as described in the section above, ''IGNITOR DOESN'T GLOW''.

Occasionally this problem can be caused by a bad thermostat. Test as described in section 2-4(c).

PILOT SYSTEM PROBLEMS

PILOT WON'T STAY LIT (PILOT SYSTEM ONLY)

If the pilot won't stay lit, the pilot & unlatch assembly is usually defective.

The pilot & unlatch assembly (figure G-5) is a safety mechanism. If there is no pilot, it closes off the gas to both the pilot and the main gas valve. This prevents accidental buildup of gas in the dryer cabinet.

The sensor is simply a bulb, like a thermometer bulb, with a liquid inside that expands when the pilot flame heats it. The liquid pushes against a metal diaphragm that holds the spring-loaded gas valve open. If the pilot goes out, the liquid cools and the diaphragm lets the spring close the gas valve.

In order to light the pilot, you must manually hold the valve open for a minute or so, until the sensor heats up enough to hold the valve open.

PILOT BURNS, BUT FLAME DOES NOT START (PILOT SYSTEM ONLY)

The gas valve solenoid coil is not opening the main gas valve. Either the gas valve solenoid coil is defective, or the burner is not getting the signal to start burning from the heating control system.

Test the wiring as described previously in the ''IGNITOR DOESN'T GLOW'' section to see if it is getting the 110-volt signal from the heating control system.

If so, the gas solenoid valve is bad. Replace it.

If the burner isn't getting 110 volts, something is wrong with the heating control system as described previously in the ''IGNITOR DOESN'T GLOW'' section.

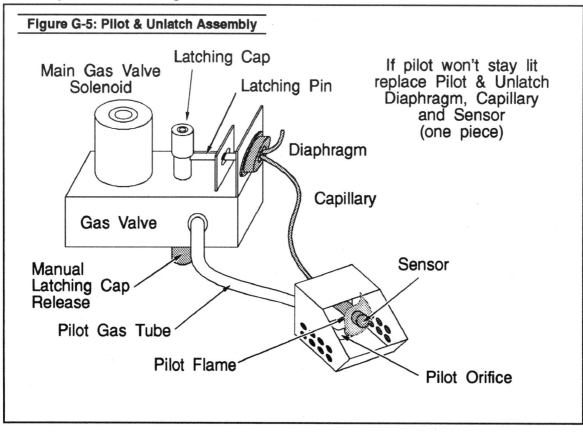

Figure G-5: Pilot & Unlatch Assembly

Main Gas Valve Solenoid

Latching Cap

Latching Pin

Diaphragm

Capillary

Gas Valve

Manual Latching Cap Release

Pilot Gas Tube

Pilot Flame

Sensor

Pilot Orifice

If pilot won't stay lit replace Pilot & Unlatch Diaphragm, Capillary and Sensor (one piece)

268,1

2-4 TESTING ELECTRICAL COMPONENTS

Sometimes you need to read a wiring diagram, to make sure you are not forgetting to check something. Sometimes you just need to find out what color wire to look for to test a component. It is ESPECIALLY important in diagnosing a bad timer.

If you already know how to read a wiring diagram, you can skip this section. If you're one of those folks who's a bit timid around electricity, all I can say is read on, and don't be too nervous. It will come to you. You learned how to use a VOM in Chapter 1, right?

Each component should be labelled clearly on your diagram. Look at figure G-6. The symbols used to represent each component are pretty universal; for example, two different symbols for thermostats are shown, but both have a little square line in them, so you know they're thermostats.

A few notes about reading a wiring diagram:

Notice that in some parts of the diagram, the lines are thicker than in other parts. The wiring and switches that are shown as thick lines are *inside* of the timer.

Also note that since heaters and ignitors are both a type of resistor, they may be shown with the resistor symbol (a zig-zag line) or they may have their own square symbol, but they should be clearly marked.

The small circles all over the diagram are terminals. These are places where you can disconnect the wire from the component for testing purposes.

If you see dotted or shaded lines around a group of wires, this is a switch assembly; for example, a temperature or cycle switch assembly. It may also be the timer, but whatever it is, it should be clearly marked on the diagram. Any wiring enclosed by a shaded or dotted box is internal to a switch assembly and must be tested as described in sections 2-4(a) and 2-4(b).

Switches may be numbered or lettered. Those markings can often be found cast or stamped into the switch. To test a switch with a certain marking, mark and disconnect all the wires from your timer. Connect your ohmmeter to the two terminal leads of the switch you want to test. For example, in figure G-6, if you want to test the hi-temp selector switch, connect one lead to the M and one to the H terminal. Then flick the switch back and forth. It should close and open. If it does, you know that contact inside the switch is good.

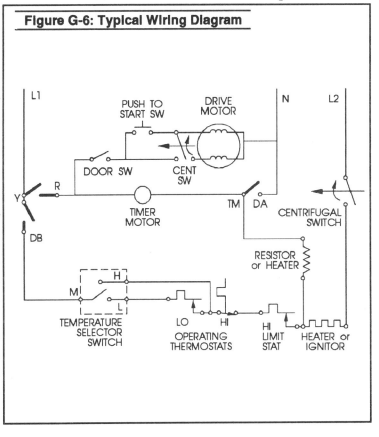

Figure G-6: Typical Wiring Diagram

Remember that for something to be energized, it must make a complete electrical circuit. You must be able to trace the path that the electricity will take, FROM the wall outlet back TO the wall outlet. This includes not only the component that you suspect, but all switches leading to it.

In Figure G-6(a), which shows a typical *electric* dryer, L1, L2, and N are the main power leads; they go directly to your wall plug. Between L1 and N, you will see 110 volts. Between L2 and N, you will also see 110 volts. But between L1 and L2, you will see 220 volts.

In gas dryers, L1 and L2 will be 110-volt leads. Sometimes they will be labelled L1 and N, but they are still 110 volt leads.

Let's say you need to check out why the heater is not working. Since a burnt out heater element is the most likely cause of this symptom, first test the heater for continuity. If you have good continuity, something else in the circuit that feeds the heater must be defective.

Following the gray-shaded circuit in figure G-6(a), note that the electricity flows from L1 to L2, so this is a 220-volt circuit.

From L1 the electricity flows to the Y-DB switch. This switch is located inside of the timer (you know this because it is drawn with thick lines) and it must be closed. The power then goes through the wire to the temperature selector switch. In this example, we have set the temperature on "low." Note that in this machine, on this setting, the electricity flows through both the high-temp and low-temp operating thermo-

stats. Therefore, both thermostats must be closed and show good continuity. The electricity then flows through the high limit thermostat, so it too must be closed and show good continuity.

The electricity flows through the heater, which we have already tested and we know is good. Then the electricity flows through the centrifugal switch, which must be closed, before going back out the main power cord (L2).

To test for the break in the circuit, simply isolate each part of the system (remove the wires from the terminals) and test for continuity. For example, to test the thermostats in our example, pull the wires off each thermostat and test continuity across the thermostat terminals as described in section 2-4(c).

The Y-DB switch is shown in bold lines, so it is inside the timer. For now, let's ignore this switch. (Remember; the timer is the *last* thing you should check; see section 2-4(b).)

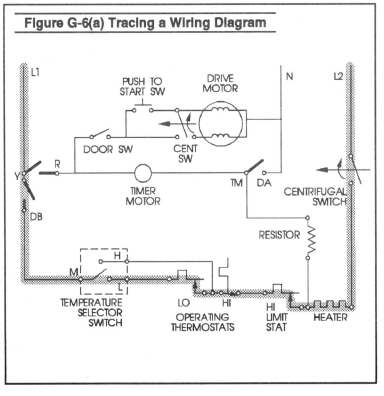

Figure G-6(a) Tracing a Wiring Diagram

That leaves the centrifugal switch, which is only closed when the motor is running. However, if you can identify the proper leads, you can use your alligator jumpers to jump across them. If you do this and the heater kicks on when you turn on the timer, you know the switch is bad.

If NONE of the other components appear to be defective, test the timer as described in section 2-4(b).

To check for a wire break, you would pull each end of a wire off the component and test for continuity through the wire. You may need to use jumpers to extend or even bypass the wire; for example, if one end of the wire is in the control console and the other end in underneath the machine. If there is no continuity, there is a break in the wire! It will then be up to you to figure out exactly where that break is; there is no magic way. If you have a broken wire, look along the length of the wire for pinching or chafing. If there is a place where the wires move , check there first. Even if the insulation is O.K., the wire may be broken inside.

2-4(a) SWITCHES AND SOLENOIDS

Testing switches and solenoids is pretty straightforward. Take all wires off the component and test resistance across it.

Switches should show good continuity when closed and no continuity when open.

Solenoids should show SOME resistance, but continuity should be good. If a solenoid shows no continuity, there's a break somewhere in the windings. If it shows no resistance, it's shorted.

2-4(b) TIMERS

The timer is the brain of the dryer. It controls everything in the cycle. In addition to telling the motor when to run, it may also activate the heating circuit or heating control circuits, humidity-sensing circuits, etc.

Solid state timers are difficult and expensive to diagnose. If you suspect a timer problem in a solid-state system, you can try replacing it, but remember that it's expensive and non-returnable (being an electrical part.) If you have one of these units that's defective, you can check into the cost of replacing it, but it's been my experience that you usually will end up just replacing the whole dryer or calling a technician. If you do call a technician, make sure you ask up front whether they work on solid-state controls.

Most timers are nothing more than a motor that drives a set of cams which open and close switches. Yet it is one of the most expensive parts in your dryer, so don't be too quick to diagnose it as the problem. Usually the FIRST thing a layman looks at is the timer; it should be the LAST. And don't forget that timers are electrical parts, which are usually non-returnable. If you buy one, and it turns out *not* to be the problem, you've just wasted the money.

In a wiring diagram, the wiring and switches that are inside the timer will usually be drawn with dark lines.

TIMER DIAGNOSIS

If the timer is not advancing *only in the automatic or humidity control cycle*, (i.e. more dry-less dry on your timer dial) see section 2-4(c) about 3-lead thermostats.

If the timer is not advancing in all cycles, well, that's pretty obvious. Replace the timer or timer drive motor, or have it rebuilt as described below.

Timers can be difficult to diagnose. The easiest way is to go through everything else in the malfunctioning system. If none of the other components are bad, then it may be the timer.

Remember that a timer is simply a set of on-off switches. The switches are turned off and on by a cam, which is driven by the timer motor. Timer wires are color-coded or number-coded.

Let's say you've got a motor starting problem. Following the shaded circuit in figure G-7, you test the door switch, push-to-start switch and centrifugal switch. They all test ok. So you think you've traced the problem to your timer.

First unplug the machine. Looking at your wiring diagram, you see that the Y-R switch feeds the drive motor. REMOVE those wires from the timer and touch the test leads to those terminals. Make sure the timer is in the ''on'' position and slowly turn the timer all the way through a full cycle. (On some timers, you cannot turn the dial while it is on. You must simply test the timer one click at a time. Be patient!)

You should see continuity make and break at least once in the cycle; usually several times. If it doesn't, the internal contacts are bad; replace the timer.

In general, timers cannot be rebuilt by the novice. Check with your parts dealer; if it *can* be rebuilt, he'll get it done for you. If it's a common one, your parts dealer may even have a rebuilt one in stock.

For the most part, if your timer is acting up, you need to replace it. To replace, mark the

wires or note the color codes written on the timer. If you need to, you can draw a picture of the terminal arrangement and wire colors. If possible, change over the timer wires one-by-one. It can be easier. If there are any special wiring changes, they will be explained in instructions that come with the new timer.

2-4(c) THERMOSTATS AND OTHER TEMPERATURE CONTROLS

THERMOSTATS (Figure G-8)

A thermostat is basically just a switch that opens or closes according to the temperature that it senses. You can test it as described in section 1-4(b) by testing for continuity across its terminals. A cold *operating* stat or *hi-limit* stat should show continuity. A cold cool-down stat should show no continuity.

This switch can be used to turn the heating system (either gas or electric) on

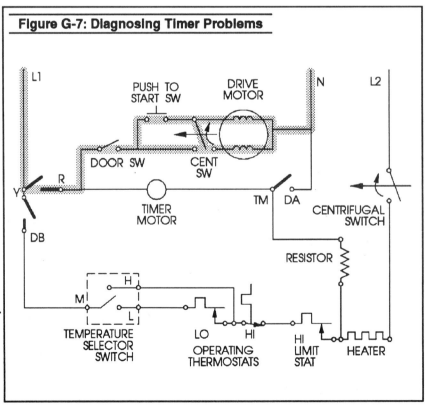

Figure G-7: Diagnosing Timer Problems

and off to maintain a certain air temperature range at a given place in the system. There may be several different thermostats side by side; for example 135 degrees for low temperature, 165 for high temperature, etc. You choose which thermostat is used by selecting the heat setting on the dryer console.

There are exceptions; for example, Frigidaire used a specially-designed thermostat that has five leads instead of two. Naturally, it is a bit more expensive than regular thermostats, and difficult to test. If you suspect it's defective, it probably is. Replace it.

3-lead thermostats are also fairly common. These thermostats are sometimes used on "automatic" drying cycles to control humidity ("more dry-less dry" on your timer dial.) These thermostats are special in that they also control the timer. When the heater is on (either gas or electric,) the timer motor is not running. When the heater kicks off, the timer advances. That's what the third lead is for. These thermostats are also difficult to test with-

out any way to heat them up. But they're pretty cheap. If the symptoms lead you to suspect that yours is defective, just replace it.

SPECIAL NOTE: In electric dryers with an automatic cycle, a special problem exists. The problem is that the heater operates on 220 volts, but the timer motor runs on 110 volts. There is a resistor in the system to cut down the voltage (see figure G-6(a) and if this resistor is bad, you will see the same symptoms as if the thermostat was bad: the timer motor will not run in the automatic cycle. If you have one of these dryers, make sure you test the resistor for continuity, in addition to the thermostat.

If a thermostat fails into a closed position, there is a danger that the heating system will continue operating until something catches fire. To prevent this, there is a high-temperature thermostat that will cut out the entire heating system.

There is no way to repair thermostats. Replace any that are bad.

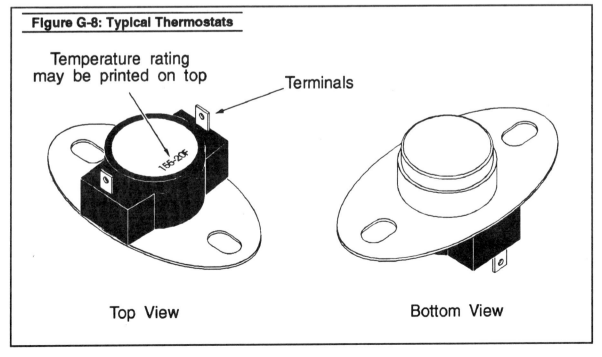

Figure G-8: Typical Thermostats

Temperature rating may be printed on top

Terminals

Top View

Bottom View

OTHER TEMPERATURE CONTROLS

Selecting which thermostat is used may be done inside the timer, or there may be a separate multi-switch that accomplishes this. Test internal timer switches as described in section 2-4(b).

Separate temperature selector switches are tested either by measuring continuity through each contact (figure G-9) or by jumping across the two correct terminals with your alligator jumpers.

2-4(d) DRIVE MOTORS AND CENTRIFUGAL START SWITCH

A motor that is trying to start, but can't for whatever reason, is using one heckuva lot of electricity. So much, in fact, that if it is allowed to continue being energized in a stalled state, it will start burning wires. To prevent this, an overload switch is installed on motors to cut power to them if they don't start within a certain amount of time.

If the motor is trying to start, but can't, you will hear certain things. First will be a click, followed immediately by a buzzing sound. Then, after about 5 to 20 seconds of buzzing, another click and the buzzing will stop. The sounds will keep repeating every minute or two. In some extreme cases, you may even smell burning.

If you hear the motor doing this, but it won't start, disconnect power and take all the load off it. For example, disconnect the drive belt, and make sure nothing is jamming the blower wheel. The motor should turn easily by hand.

Try to start the motor again. If it still won't start, the motor is bad. If you have an ammeter, the stalled motor will be drawing 10 to 20 amps or more.

STARTING SWITCH

Dryers have a centrifugal starting switch mounted piggyback on the motor. There are many sets of contacts inside the switch, and each design is different, even among dryers of the same brand. Testing the switch is most easily accomplished by replacing it.

Remember that starting switches are electrical parts, which are generally not returnable. If you test the switch by replacing it, and the problem turns out to be the motor itself, you will probably not be able to return the starting switch for a refund. But they're pretty cheap, and if it *is* the problem, you just saved yourself the best part of a hundred bucks for a new motor.

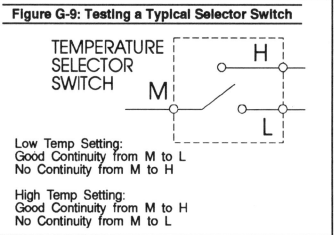

Figure G-9: Testing a Typical Selector Switch

TEMPERATURE SELECTOR SWITCH

Low Temp Setting:
Good Continuity from M to L
No Continuity from M to H

High Temp Setting:
Good Continuity from M to H
No Continuity from M to L

If the motor is stalled (buzzing and/or tripping out on the overload switch) and the starting switch tests O.K., the motor is bad. Replace it.

NOTE: Many motors have the belt pulley pressed onto the motor shaft. However, a replacement motor may come without a pulley. When buying a new motor, make sure that the pulley can be changed over, or else get a new pulley with the new motor. It may save you a second trip to the parts dealer.

2-4(e) IGNITORS

You can test the ignitor by testing for resistance across the element. (See figure G-10) A good ignitor will show quite a bit of resistance, between about 50 and 600 ohms. A bad ignitor will usually show no continuity at all.

2-4(f) ELECTRIC HEATERS

Electric heater elements are tested by measuring continuity across them. Like ignitors, they should show quite a bit of resistance, and defective heaters will usually show no continuity at all.

2-5 AIRFLOW

Airflow is extremely important in every dryer. Any blockage can cause slow drying or no drying. It can come on suddenly (like if something happens to the dryer vent outside the house) or it can show up as a progressive problem, as lint slowly builds up in the dryer exhaust system.

First, check the lint screen. It seems obvious to you and me, but don't take it for granted. Check the screen yourself, regardless of who else says they've checked it. I ran into one old gentleman who'd been widowed *ten months before*. His only problem was a clogged lint screen (we're talkin'

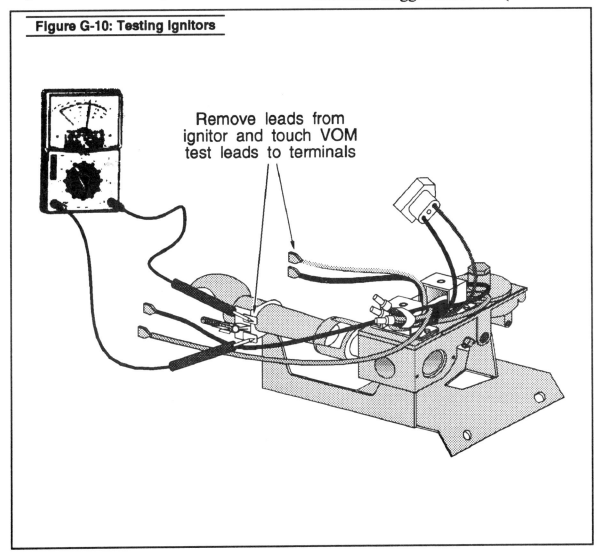

Figure G-10: Testing Ignitors

Remove leads from ignitor and touch VOM test leads to terminals

clogged here; the lint was literally about two inches thick on the screen.) His wife had always done the laundry, and he simply didn't know that he had to clean the screen. I think it's a tribute to Whirlpool engineering that the thing was still running at all with that much lint in it.

If the lint screen is clean, check the exhaust system between the dryer and the house outlet. A really easy way is to disconnect the exhaust system and run the dryer for a few minutes with it venting directly into the house. If the dryer functions normally, the exhaust system is clogged.

If none of the above works, the internal ducting or blower fan is clogged or malfunctioning. To open the dryer and clean out the ducting, see the chapter about your brand.

NOTE: Many models CAN be operated with the front of the cabinet taken off, but since there is nothing enclosing the dryer drum, there will be no airflow, and the heating system will not operate properly. In fact, doing this will overheat the heating system.

2-6 DRIVE BELTS AND TENSIONERS

To access the drive belt, see the chapter about your brand.

If you see any of the problems pictured in figure G-11, replace the belt.

It is important for the belt tensioner to be operating properly. Check for broken springs. Also check that the tensioner idler roller spins freely.

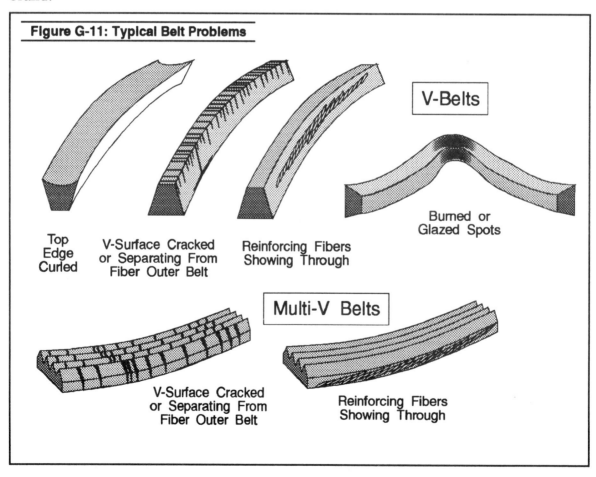

Figure G-11: Typical Belt Problems

V-Belts

Top Edge Curled

V-Surface Cracked or Separating From Fiber Outer Belt

Reinforcing Fibers Showing Through

Burned or Glazed Spots

Multi-V Belts

V-Surface Cracked or Separating From Fiber Outer Belt

Reinforcing Fibers Showing Through

Chapter 3

WHIRLPOOL / KENMORE

3-1 MACHINE LAYOUT

Figure W-1 shows the general layout of these machines.

The drum is supported at the front by a slider around the inside lip of the drum, and at the rear by support rollers.

The blower fan is attached directly to the rear of the drive motor. The drive belt comes directly off the front of the motor and goes completely around the drum.

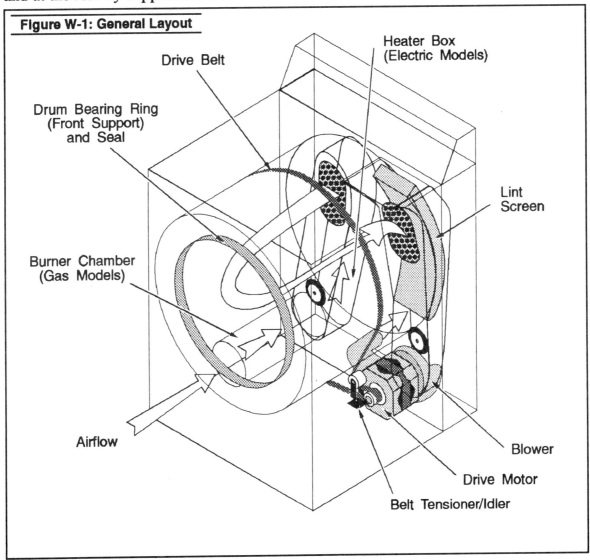

Figure W-1: General Layout

Drive Belt

Heater Box (Electric Models)

Drum Bearing Ring (Front Support) and Seal

Lint Screen

Burner Chamber (Gas Models)

Airflow

Blower

Drive Motor

Belt Tensioner/Idler

3-2 COMMON PROBLEMS

The two most common problems in these machines are:

1) Noisy operation, usually a loud rumbling sound getting progressively worse over time, caused by worn drum support rollers. Usually this appears in machines about 7-15 years old. To replace the rollers, remove the drum as described in section 3-3.

2) No heat, caused by a broken ignitor. See chapter 2, section 2-3(a) to replace.

If you hear a loud, regular clackety-clacking as the dryer drum is turning, and you do not have any metal zippers or buttons inside the drum, some coins may have gotten inside the vanes. Look inside the dryer drum. One of the three tumbling vanes will be plastic. Turn the drum until the plastic vane is on top. Open the top of the cabinet as shown in figure W-2. Remove the screws that hold the vane in place and remove any coins that have gotten in the vanes.

Another fairly common problem is that the dryer door support cables break. See figure W-3 for a cross section of the cable mechanism. To access the cables, lift the top of the cabinet and remove the kickplate. In models without a kickplate, you will need to remove the front of the cabinet as described in section 3-3.

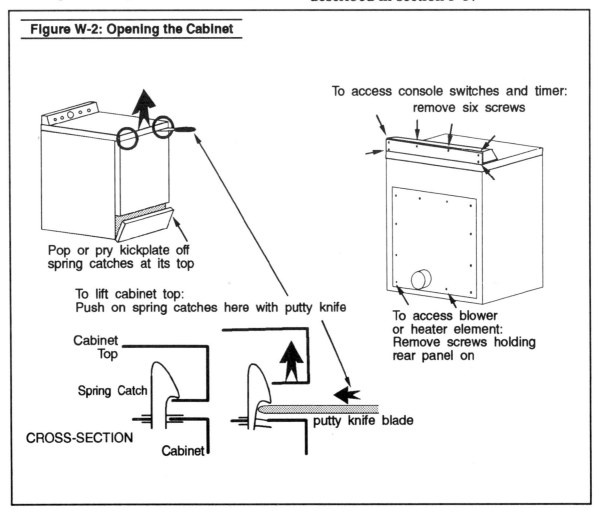

Figure W-2: Opening the Cabinet

Pop or pry kickplate off spring catches at its top

To lift cabinet top:
Push on spring catches here with putty knife

Cabinet Top

Spring Catch

CROSS-SECTION

Cabinet

putty knife blade

To access console switches and timer:
remove six screws

To access blower or heater element:
Remove screws holding rear panel on

3-3 DRUM REMOVAL

Unplug the machine and move it away from the wall far enough so the console will not hit the wall when you raise the cabinet top.

Lift the lint screen access cover and remove the two screws inside.

NOTE: Do not remove the lint screen unless necessary, and only after removing the screws. This will prevent your accidentally dropping the screws down the lint screen slot. If you accidentally drop anything down the lint screen slot, it goes right into the blower wheel. If this happens, see section 3-5 for access to the blower wheel.

Lift the top of the cabinet as shown in figure W-2. If you have a model with a kickplate, remove the kickplate, too.

If you have a kickplate model, remove the belt from the motor pinion. The easiest way is to push the belt tensioner to loosen the belt with your thumb, and use the fingers of the same hand to slip the loop of belt off the motor pinion. (See figure W-5)

Loosen (but don't remove) the bottom screws holding the front of the cabinet on. Remove the two top screws inside the cabinet that hold on the cabinet front.

CAUTION: Remember that the front of the cabinet supports the front of the dryer drum! Remove the cabinet front carefully!

Balance the whole shebang against your knees and disconnect the wire leads from the door switch. Hold the dryer drum in place and lift the front of the cabinet off.

NOTE: In certain drop-door models, (known in the parts houses as "hamper-door" models) there may be a couple of extra screws holding on the front of the cabinet, in the middle of the hinges.

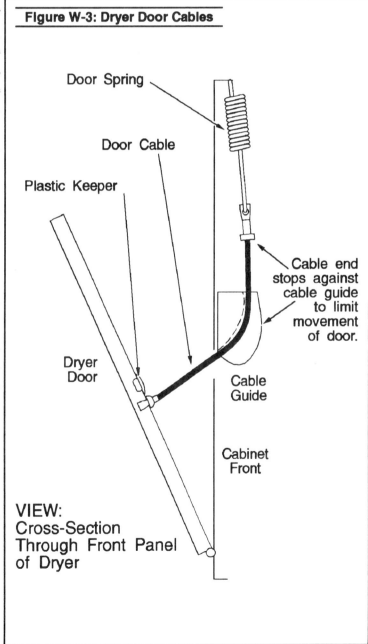

Figure W-3: Dryer Door Cables

Door Spring

Door Cable

Plastic Keeper

Cable end stops against cable guide to limit movement of door.

Dryer Door

Cable Guide

Cabinet Front

VIEW: Cross-Section Through Front Panel of Dryer

To remove the dryer drum from the cabinet:

1) In kickplate models, you have already removed the belt tension, so slide the drum straight outward through the curved cutouts in the cabinet sides. (See figure W-4)

2) In models without a kickplate, you must hold the dryer drum in place while you reach beneath it to remove the belt tension as described previously. It takes a little acrobatics, but it isn't *too* tough.

The drum support rollers will now be easily accessible. (See figure W-4) The one on the left tends to be worn more than the other one, but replace them both. When replacing, use only ONE drop of oil on the hub. Oil tends to attract dust and lint, and over-oiling them can actually shorten the life of them.

While you have the dryer dismantled, vacuum out all the dust you can. Also, it's a good idea to replace the belt and belt tensioner whenever you have the dryer dismantled to this point. It is cheap insurance against future problems.

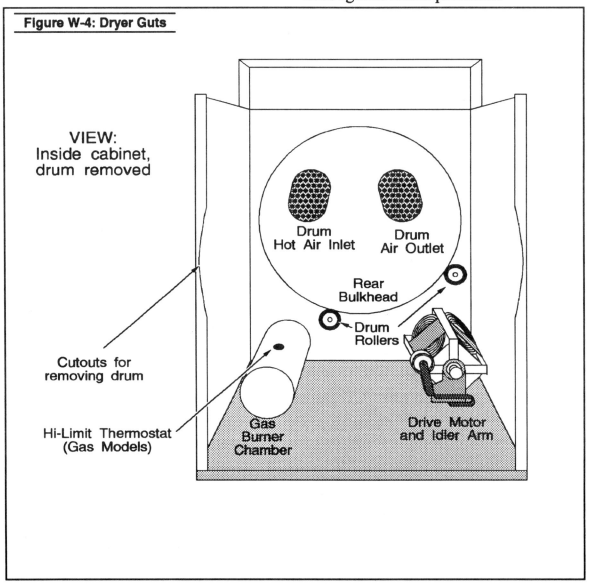

Figure W-4: Dryer Guts

VIEW:
Inside cabinet,
drum removed

Drum
Hot Air Inlet

Drum
Air Outlet

Rear
Bulkhead

Drum
Rollers

Cutouts for
removing drum

Hi-Limit Thermostat
(Gas Models)

Gas
Burner
Chamber

Drive Motor
and Idler Arm

HINT: Coins that find their way out the rear drum seal tend to end up directly beneath the left drum roller. I found eight bucks worth of quarters in one machine!

Inspect the rear drum seal (attached to the back of the dryer drum.) If it is badly worn, replace it. Your parts dealer will have a seal kit, and it is actually quite inexpensive and easy to glue a new one in place.

Re-assembly is basically the opposite of disassembly.

Installing the drum can be a bit tricky, especially if you don't have a kickplate machine. Make sure the belt is around the drum before you put the drum in place. Before you put the cabinet front on, reach beneath the drum and make sure the two rollers are in the groove of the drum. If you have a kickplate machine, you can install the cabinet front at this time. If you don't have a machine with a kickplate, you have to line up and put tension on the belt *before* you put on the cabinet front.

When the drum is in place, make sure the belt is flat on the drum and closely line up the belt on on the old belt skid mark on the drum. To tension the belt, make a loop of belt and stick it under the tensioner as shown in figure W-5. Push the tensioner with your thumb and slip the belt loop around the motor pinion.

After installing the dryer front, roll the dryer drum around several times by hand. As you turn it, check that the belt is flat all the way around. Also check that the rear drum seal is flat all the way around, and not pinched between the drum and the rear support plate.

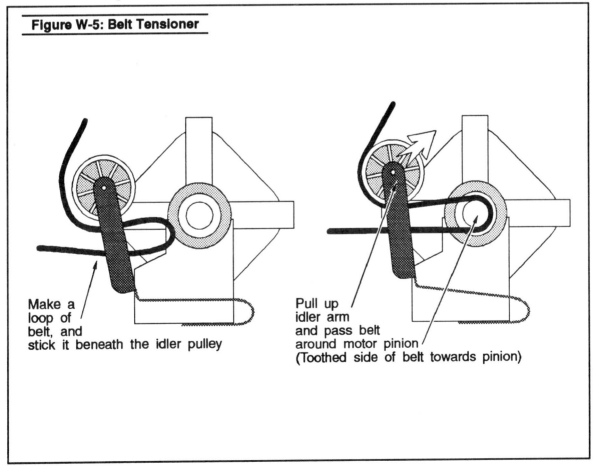

Figure W-5: Belt Tensioner

Make a loop of belt, and stick it beneath the idler pulley

Pull up idler arm and pass belt around motor pinion (Toothed side of belt towards pinion)

3-4 REPLACING THE HEATER ELEMENT (ELECTRIC MODELS)

The heater element is accessed through the back of the dryer, as shown in figure W-6.

The heater elements are located inside the riser on the right, as you look at the back of the machine. You can test it for continuity without removing it. To remove the riser, raise the top of the cabinet and disconnect the strap that holds the top of the riser.

3-5 ACCESS TO THE BLOWER WHEEL OR THERMOSTATS

To get to the blower wheel, remove the back of the dryer as shown in figure W-6.

The blower wheel is under the bottom of the lint screen duct to your left, as you look at the back of the dryer.

The operating thermostats are at the blower wheel outlet.

In electric models, the hi-temperature cutout thermostat is mounted to the heat riser; in gas models, on top of the burner chamber.

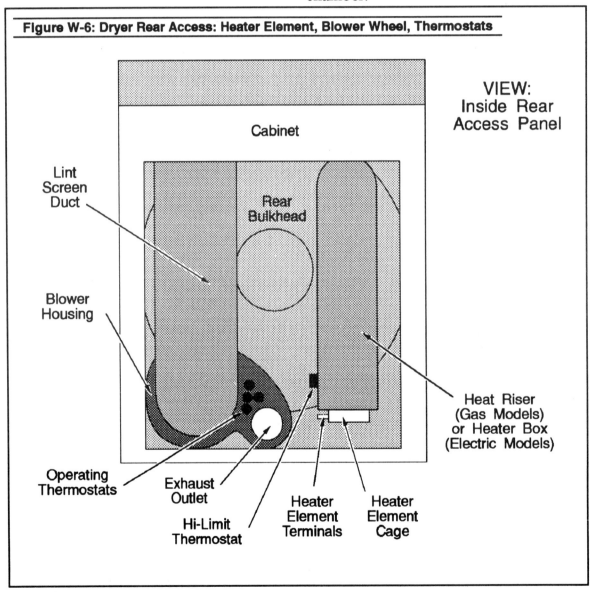

Figure W-6: Dryer Rear Access: Heater Element, Blower Wheel, Thermostats

Chapter 4

GENERAL ELECTRIC

4-1 MACHINE LAYOUT

Figure GE-1 shows the general layout of these machines.

The front of the drum is supported by two small glide pads. The rear of the drum is supported by a small shaft and bearing, which is accessible through a small plate in the rear of the machine.

The blower fan is attached directly to the front of the drive motor. The drive belt comes directly off the rear of the motor and goes completely around the drum.

Electrical model GE dryers use a double heater element. *One* of the two elements is energized for the low heat cycle; *both* heaters are energized for high heat. Late models have the heater elements contained in a cylindrical heater chamber fastened to the right front baseplate of the machine. In earlier models, the heaters are in a circular chamber directly behind the drum.

Figure GE-1: General Layout

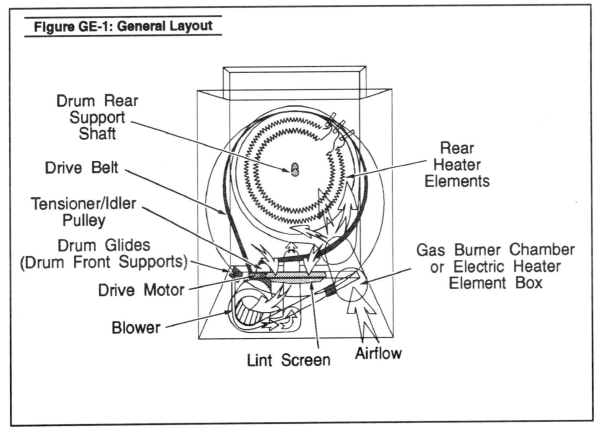

Drum Rear Support Shaft

Drive Belt

Tensioner/Idler Pulley

Drum Glides (Drum Front Supports)

Drive Motor

Blower

Rear Heater Elements

Gas Burner Chamber or Electric Heater Element Box

Lint Screen

Airflow

GE went kind of crazy with thermostats for a while. I'm sure their design engineers know what they're doing, but...well, let's just say that to my experience, GE machines tend to have more thermostats than other brands. Moreover, they tend to migrate from model to model. Your model may have thermostats in just about any of the places shown in figure GE-2.

4-2 COMMON PROBLEMS

The most common problems with these machines are:

1) Noisy operation. If you hear a very loud clattering sound, the belt could be broken. When the belt breaks in these machines, the tensioner touches the motor pulley and causes one heckuva loud racket. To confirm this diagnosis, check to see if the drum is turning. Replace the belt as described in section 4-3.

Another common cause of noise happens when the drum front support glides wear out. This causes a pronounced scrubbing sound (metal-to-metal.) Also, if they are worn badly, you will see the top inner lip of the drum wearing the inside top of the clothes port. The solution is to remove the front of the cabinet as described in section 4-3 and replace the drum front support glides .

A squeaking or squealing noise can be caused by the rear drum bearing wearing out. Remove the drum and replace the bearing as described in section 4-4.

2) Heating problems. Diagnose and repair as described in Chapter 2.

4-3 CABINET ACCESS PANELS (Fig. GE-3)

ACCESS TO BELT TENSIONER, REAR BEARING OR GAS BURNER

Each of these components has its own access panel:

The gas burner access panel is located in the lower right front of the cabinet. To open, push in on the top of the panel. The bottom is on nylon snaps and will pop off. Then just lift the panel out.

The belt tensioner is accessed through the bottom panel of the back of the dryer.

The rear drum support bearing is accessed through the small panel in the center of the back of the dryer.

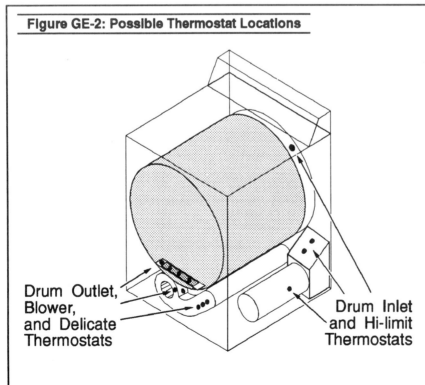

Figure GE-2: Possible Thermostat Locations

Drum Outlet, Blower, and Delicate Thermostats

Drum Inlet and Hi-limit Thermostats

CABINET FRONT PANEL AND DRUM GLIDES

Two different methods were used to fasten the front panel to the cabinet top (figure GE-3). Unscrew the screws or pop the catches and lift the lid of the dryer.

NOTE: If you are testing the heaters of rear-heater models, the terminals are accessible at this point. Look to the rear of the drum on the right side. You can test them as described in section 4-6. In bottom-heater models, you must remove the front panel as described below to test the heater element.

Loosen, but do not remove, the two screws at the bottom front corners of the front panel of the cabinet.

Unscrew the two screws at the top front corners inside the cabinet. Disconnect any door switch wires and lift off the front panel of the dryer.

You can replace the belt at this point, without removing the drum. Release the belt tension as described in section 4-4. You can slip the belt between the drum and the glides.

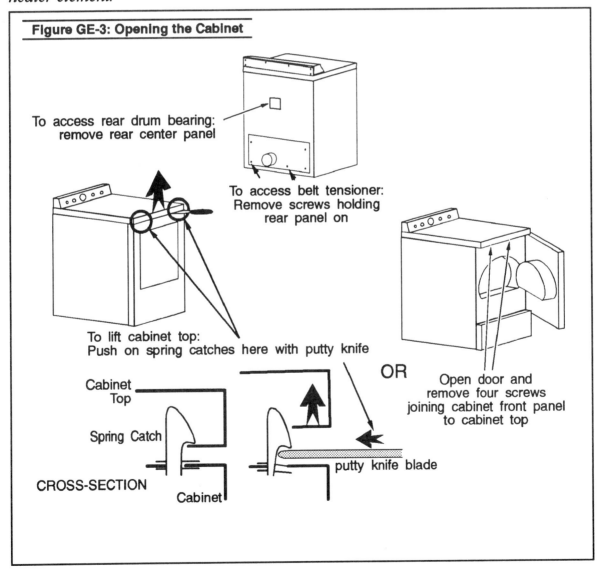

Figure GE-3: Opening the Cabinet

To access rear drum bearing: remove rear center panel

To access belt tensioner: Remove screws holding rear panel on

To lift cabinet top: Push on spring catches here with putty knife

Open door and remove four screws joining cabinet front panel to cabinet top

OR

Cabinet Top

Spring Catch

CROSS-SECTION

Cabinet

putty knife blade

Once the cabinet front panel is off, inspect the blower wheel at the lower left corner of the dryer for foreign debris, excessive lint or broken blades. The blower hub has a two-piece clamp which will fall apart if you remove it, so do not remove the hub clamp unless you plan to remove the whole motor and blower housing assembly as described in section 4-4.

Also while the cabinet front panel is off, inspect the felt seal inside the front panel for wear, excessive lint, or any debris that might be stuck to it.

Remove and inspect the front drum support glides as shown in figure GE-4. Whether they're badly worn or not, it's a good idea to replace them as cheap insurance against future problems.

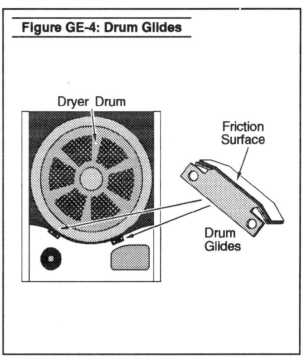

Figure GE-4: Drum Glides

Dryer Drum

Friction Surface

Drum Glides

Figure GE-5: Belt Tensioner

Drive Belt

Tension Spring

Idler Pulley

Drive Motor

Idler Arm

Motor Pinion

4-4 DRUM REMOVAL

The drum must be removed to service the electric heaters, to remove the blower or motor, to replace the rear drum bearing, or to replace the heater elements in electric models.

Open the rear cabinet bottom panel. Reach inside and remove the belt tension as shown in figure GE-5.

Remove the small inspection plate in the center of the rear of the dryer. Inside, you will see the drum support shaft and an "E-"ring holding it in place. Remove the "E-"ring with a small screwdriver. If you have a magnet, you may also be able to use it to avoid dropping the ring inside the dryer.

There are spacer shims between the bearing and the "E-"ring. There are more shims inside the bearing, between the bearing and the drum. Some are nylon and some are metal. Note how they come off, and make sure you put the shims back on the same way they come off.

Remove the cabinet front panel as described in section 4-3. In certain models, you will also need to remove the front drum support glides to get the drum out.

Once the cabinet front panel is off, you should be able to lift and slide the dryer drum straight outward.

While the machine is open, vacuum out all accumulated lint. Be careful not to knock any wires loose.

4-5 BLOWER SERVICE

If you need to replace the blower wheel, you must remove the dryer drum as described in section 4-4. Pull the six screws holding the blower housing to the baseplate, remove the motor mounting nuts and pull out the motor and blower housing as an assembly. In some models, you must remove the tensioner arm to get the motor assembly out.

When re-installing the blower, you must align the blower wheel so it does not touch the blower housing. To do this, loosen (but do not remove!) the clamp that holds the wheel to the motor shaft.

4-6 ELECTRIC HEATERS

The heater elements can be tested without removing them. Note which lead goes on which terminal and remove the leads from the terminals. The two heater elements are tested separately, if *one* is bad, *BOTH* must be replaced. Test them as described in Chapter 2. The elements are wired as shown in figure GE-6.

In rear-heater (circular) models, the elements must be pre-stretched to the correct length before installing. Follow the instructions that come with the new heaters. DO NOT OVERSTRETCH THEM! It's better to leave them an inch or so short, and work them to the proper length when the heater element is in place in the dryer. Also, make sure you inspect the porcelain insulators and replace any that are cracked or broken.

In bottom heater models, the whole heater chamber is replaced. Remove the two screws holding down the front end of the chamber and the back end just slips out of the heat riser.

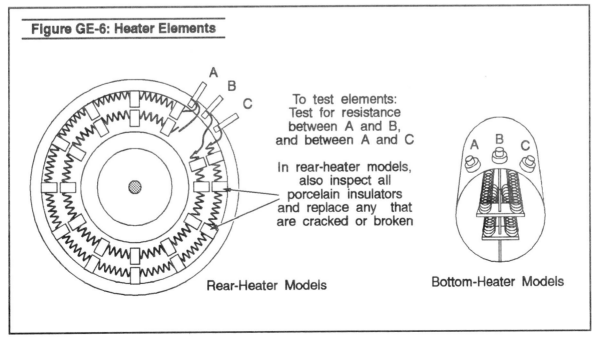

Figure GE-6: Heater Elements

To test elements:
Test for resistance between A and B, and between A and C

In rear-heater models, also inspect all porcelain insulators and replace any that are cracked or broken

Rear-Heater Models

Bottom-Heater Models

Chapter 5

OLD-STYLE MAYTAG ("Halo of Heat" Models)

In the mid 1980's, Maytag began selling a completely redesigned dryer. Prior to that, they sold a design called a "halo of heat" model. These older machines were well-built and there are still a vast number of them in service.

The easiest way to tell them apart is that in the "halo" models, the lint screen is inside the center rear of the drum, whereas the late model Maytag machines have the lint screen in the front of the cabinet, at the bottom of the door opening.

5-1 MACHINE LAYOUT

The "halo of heat" name comes from the fact that in electric models, there is a single circular heater element around the front of the drum. The "halo" actually encircles the front door opening.

There are no front drum supports in these machines; the drum is completely supported by the shaft at the rear of the drum. The blower housing in these machines is a structural member and it contains the bearings that support the drum shaft. A frame (called a "spider") holds up the blower housing. (Figure MH-1) The blower wheel itself is concentric with the drum and runs on the drum shaft.

There are two belts at the rear of these machines. One comes off the drive motor and drives the blower and a tensioner/idler. The second runs from the tensioner/idler and drives the drum.

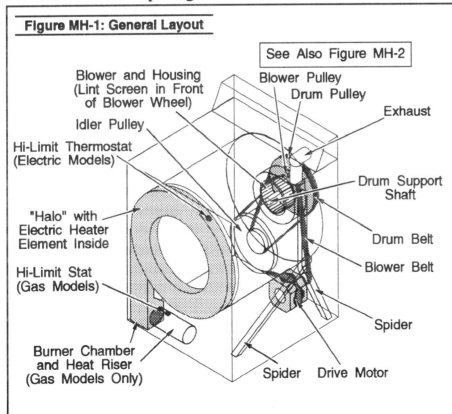

Figure MH-1: General Layout

See Also Figure MH-2

Blower and Housing (Lint Screen in Front of Blower Wheel)

Idler Pulley

Hi-Limit Thermostat (Electric Models)

"Halo" with Electric Heater Element Inside

Hi-Limit Stat (Gas Models)

Burner Chamber and Heat Riser (Gas Models Only)

Blower Pulley

Drum Pulley

Exhaust

Drum Support Shaft

Drum Belt

Blower Belt

Spider

Spider   Drive Motor

All gas models have pilot ignition. None have electric or glo-type ignitors. The gas burner and burner chamber on these machines runs across the bottom front of the baseplate, with the gas valve on the right and the heat riser duct on the left. Access to the valve is through a burner inspection cover on the lower right front of the machine.

The heating control system is slightly different in these machines, especially in electronic control models. They are set up to sense the moisture in the clothes using humidity sensors in the baffles (vanes) inside the drum. Once the proper humidity is reached inside the drum, the heating system shuts down, but the cool-down thermostat keeps the motor running until the clothes cool off a bit. Failure of this system can cause a few odd symptoms as described in section 5-2.

The operating thermostats in these machines are located on top of the blower housing, inside the back of the machine. If there are two thermostats in that location, the one on the right is a cool-down thermostat and should be *open* when cold. The hi-limit thermostat is located at the top of the halo on electric models, and on top of the burner chamber on gas models.

5-2 COMMON PROBLEMS

The most common problems with these machines are:

1) The belts wear out or break. The symptom is that the drum does not turn. If you replace one belt, you must replace them both or the machine will not run right. See section 5-3 to replace.

2) In gas models, there is a problem when the cabinet feels uncomfortably hot to the touch. The front felt seals deteriorate or burn, and hot air escapes straight from the halo into the cabinet. To replace them, you must remove the whole cabinet from the machine as described in section 5-4.

3) The bearing on the blower wheel seizes, and the blower wheel locks up. The symptom is that the exhaust will be weak or non-existent, and usually the dryer drum won't turn. Replace the blower wheel as described in section 5-3.

4) Heating problems. Diagnose and repair as described in Chapter 2. Electric heater elements can be tested by removing the cabinet as described in section 5-4.

5) In electronic control models, the motor sometimes will not shut off. The heat also keeps cycling on and off long past when the clothes are dry. This is usually caused by the humidity sensors within the drum being gummed up with starch or other deposits. The sensors look like copper wires or silver bars imbedded into the baffles (vanes) of the dryer drum. If your dryer won't shut off, try cleaning the baffles. You may have to scrape a little, but be careful not to damage the sensors imbedded into the vane.

6) If the motor doesn't shut off, but the heat *has* stopped cycling on and off, the cool-down thermostat may be stuck in a closed position. (The cool-down is the thermostat on the right, as you look into the back of the dryer.) The heating system shuts down when the humidity sensors sense that the clothes are dry, and these thermostats keep the motor running for a short time after that

to cool down the clothes. Unlike other thermostats, these cool-down thermostats should be *open* when the dryer is cool. If they are *closed* when cool, the contacts inside are welded shut and the motor won't stop running. Test the thermostat and replace if you suspect it's defective.

The same symptom may be caused by the machine not being grounded. These machines MUST be grounded, either through the third prong of the wall plug or directly from the cabinet to a house ground. If you have recently moved the machine, and now it won't shut off, check to make sure the machine is grounded somehow.

7) In very early machines, the motor pulley was made of a pot metal material. Strange symptom, but the *belt* can actually wear out the *pulley*. If this happens, the proper belt tension cannot be maintained and the dryer drum will turn very weakly. These pot metal pullies are easily recognized, as they had a greenish color. Replace it with a steel pulley, available at your parts dealer.

5-3 REAR ACCESS, BELT REPLACEMENT, BLOWER SERVICE

To change the belts or blower wheel, open the rear panel by removing the screws that hold it on.

The idler pulley on the lower right, as you look in the back of the dryer, (figure MH-2) is spring loaded and keeps tension on the belts. Remove the tension spring to remove the belts.

Once the belts are removed, check that both the idler and drum pullies are turning freely, without binding.

To get to the blower wheel, remove the drum pulley. The small pulley beneath is the blower pulley, which is one piece with the blower wheel. Try turning this pulley by hand around the drum shaft. If it is binding, replace the blower wheel.

To remove the blower wheel, First remove the exhaust elbow. Then remove the blower housing cover screws and the cover will come off the housing.

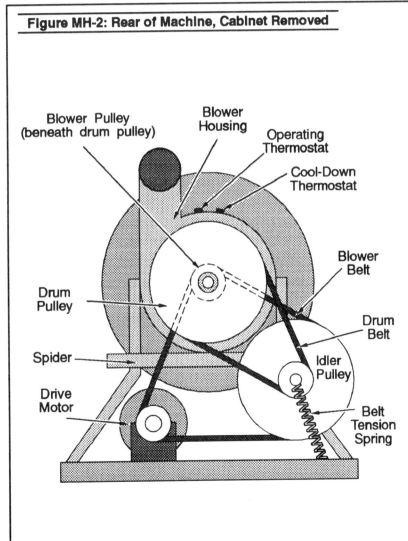

Figure MH-2: Rear of Machine, Cabinet Removed

Blower Pulley (beneath drum pulley)

Blower Housing

Operating Thermostat

Cool-Down Thermostat

Drum Pulley

Spider

Drive Motor

Blower Belt

Drum Belt

Idler Pulley

Belt Tension Spring

5-4 ACCESS TO THE HALO AREA

To test or replace the electric heating elements, door switch, or felt seal, you must remove the entire cabinet.

Unplug the dryer and remove the back as described in section 5-3.

Disconnect the motor wiring harness plug at the motor. Remove the harness from any routing clips holding it to the spider. Also disconnect the wire leads to the operating thermostats.

Remove the two cabinet mounting screws at the bottom rear corners of the dryer. Also remove the three screws at the bottom of each side of the cabinet; these hold the cabinet to the baseplate.

In gas models, the halo is connected to the baseplate of the dryer and stays with it when you remove the cabinet. In electric models, the halo comes off with the cabinet. Therefore, in gas models, you must also remove the four screws from inside the dryer door (Figure MH-3) that connect the halo to the cabinet front.

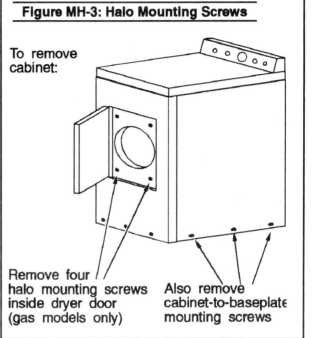

Figure MH-3: Halo Mounting Screws

To remove cabinet:

Remove four halo mounting screws inside dryer door (gas models only)

Also remove cabinet-to-baseplate mounting screws

You can now lift the cabinet off. Be careful, it is heavy. Also take care that the wiring harnesses don't get tangled up in anything as the cabinet comes off.

In gas models, there is a felt seal between the halo and the drum. (Figure MH-4) The seal has two pieces; the seal itself, and a felt band which keeps the seal in tension around the drum. Inspect it for burning or damage. A seal kit is available from your parts dealer. To replace, remove the halo.

In electric models, inspect the heater element and test it for continuity. Replace if defective. Also check the insulators that hold the element in place for cracking and replace if defective.

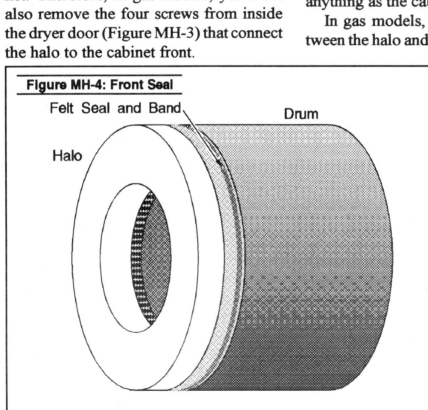

Figure MH-4: Front Seal

Felt Seal and Band

Drum

Halo

Chapter 6

LATE MODEL MAYTAG

In the mid-1980's, Maytag began selling a completely redesigned dryer. Prior to that, they sold a design called a ''halo of heat'' model. (See Chapter 5)

The easiest way to tell them apart is that in the ''halo'' models, the lint screen is inside the center rear of the drum, whereas the late model Maytag machines have the lint screen in the front of the cabinet, at the bottom of the door opening.

6-1 MACHINE LAYOUT

Figure ML-1 shows the general layout of these machines.

The drum is supported at the front by two small glides beneath the drum. The rear of the drum is supported by rollers.

The cabinet is solid on three sides, so almost everything is accessed through the front of the machine. There is a small inspection panel on the bottom right, as you look at the back of the machine, through which you can get to the belt tensioner and idler pulley.

The blower fan is mounted directly to the front of the drive motor. The drive pulley and belt come off the rear of the motor, and the belt goes completely around the drum. The motor and blower are on the left side of the baseplate of the machine. A spring-loaded idler, mounted to the motor baseplate, keeps tension on the belt.

In gas models the burner is on the right side of the baseplate of the machine. It is accessible through the small inspection door on the lower right front of the machine. In electric models, the heater is located in a cylindrical heater box in the same place as the burner chamber.

Figure ML-1: General Layout

Drum Rollers (Rear Supports)

Heat Riser

Drive Belt

Drum Glides (Drum Front Supports)

Drive Motor

Blower

Lint Screen

Gas Burner Chamber or Electric Heater Element Box

Airflow

Operating thermostats in these machines are located on the front of the blower exhaust housing. Hi-limit stats are located on top of the burner chamber in gas models, and directly on top of the heater box in electric models.

6-2 COMMON PROBLEMS

The most common problems in these machines are as follows:

1) Loud rumbling or banging noise, getting progressively worse over time, or squeaky sounds coming from the drum support rollers. Replace as described in section 6-4.

2) Heating problems as described in chapter 2.

3) Drum doesn't turn, caused by a broken belt. Replace as described in section 6-4.

4) No airflow. These machines seem to be particularly susceptible to getting clogged up with lint. Remove the front panel and clean out the blower as described in section 6-3.

5) These machines seem to be susceptible to things slipping past the lint screen, especially pens and pencils and such. If this happens, you will hear a loud grinding sound that seems like it resounds through the whole machine. Open the blower cover and inspect the blower wheel as described in section 6-3. Replace the blower wheel if the blades are chewed up.

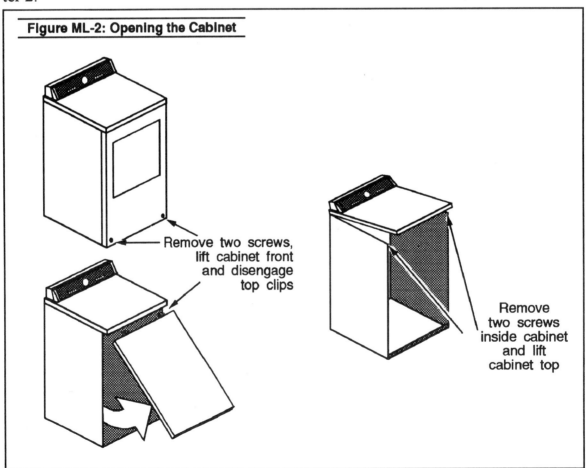

Figure ML-2: Opening the Cabinet

Remove two screws, lift cabinet front and disengage top clips

Remove two screws inside cabinet and lift cabinet top

6-3 OPENING THE CABINET (Figure ML-2)

Remove the two screws at the bottom of the cabinet front. Lift the bottom of the front panel until the clips at the top of the panel disengage from the top. Be careful to note the position of any door switch or other wiring and disconnect it as you remove the panel.

To lift the cabinet top, remove the two screws beneath the front corners.

BLOWER

To inspect, clean or replace the blower wheel, remove the blower inlet cover. The blower wheel is held onto the motor shaft with a spring clip.

6-4 DRUM REMOVAL

To inspect and/or replace drum glides, belts or electric heater elements, you must remove the drum as follows:

1) Open the inspection panel on the back of the machine and release belt tension.

2) Remove the cabinet front as described in section 6-3.

3) Remove the four screws from the front bulkhead as shown in figure ML-3. While holding the drum in place, lift out the bulkhead and set it aside. You can now lift out the drum.

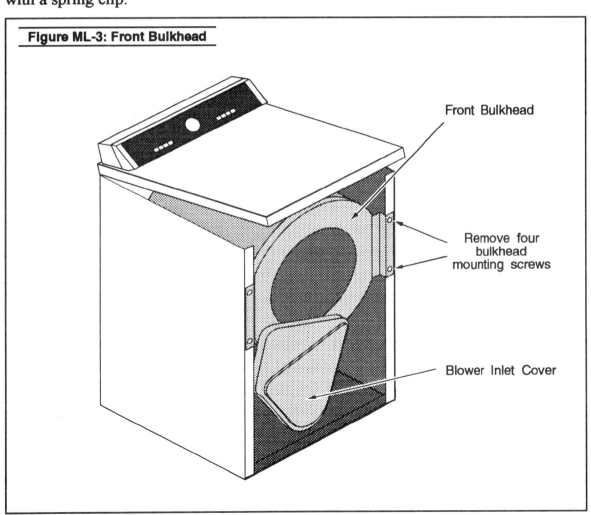

Figure ML-3: Front Bulkhead

Front Bulkhead

Remove four bulkhead mounting screws

Blower Inlet Cover

The drum glides are on the lower front corners of the inside of the bulkhead. They are riveted in place. If you need to change them, you must drill out the rivets and rivet new ones in place. The rivets come with the glide kit.

The drum support roller shafts are held onto the rear bulkhead with a nut. (Figure ML-4) Remove the nut to remove the roller wheels.

The front and rear drum seals can also be inspected for wear at this point. They are glued onto the front and back bulkheads. If you need to replace them, you must scrape off the old adhesive and glue in new ones.

In electric models, the heater element is located inside the heater box on the right side of the baseplate of the machine. Test it for continuity as described in Chapter 2, and if defective, replace the heater box.

Don't forget to check that the idler rolls smoothly. Replace if sticking or binding, by pulling off the spring clip that holds the idler pulley to its shaft.

BELT REPLACEMENT

Getting the belt around the idler in these machines can be a real son-of-a-gun. For one thing, the belt is sort of upside-down compared to other machines; the flat side goes against the drum and idler. (See figure ML-5) There's also a lot of spring tension.

Try to position the belt as closely as possible on the old skid marks on the drum. And after you get it on, slowly rotate the drum a few times to make sure the belt doesn't jump off the idler.

Figure ML-4: Rear Bulkhead and Drum Rollers

Rear Bulkhead

Drum Rollers are held to rear bulkhead by nut on back side of bulkhead.

Figure ML-5: Drive Belt Tensioner

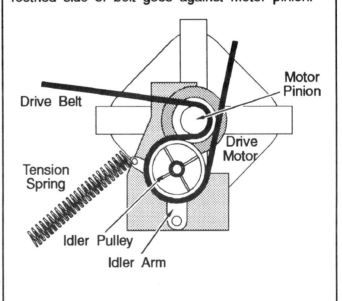

Note: Flat side of belt goes against drum and idler pulley.

Toothed side of belt goes against motor pinion.

Drive Belt

Motor Pinion

Drive Motor

Tension Spring

Idler Pulley

Idler Arm

Chapter 7

OLD-STYLE NORGE

All through the 60's and 70's, and into the 80's, Norge produced a rather peculiar design, compared with other brands. The most unique feature of the design was that there was a very large blower fan, nearly as large in diameter as the drum itself, situated directly behind the drum. This fan takes suction directly from the heater, and *blows* air into the drum; thus, unlike most other dryer designs, the drum is under *pressure*. All models are supported at the rear by a shaft at the center of the drum. Early models have rollers supporting the front of the drum; later models have glides. These machines were pretty well built; there are still substantial numbers of them in service.

7-1 MACHINE LAYOUT

Very early models had a single V-belt at the rear of the machine. The belt goes from the drive motor to a pulley in the center of the machine which drives the fan. It also goes to a second pulley in the lower left rear of the machine. This pulley is shafted to the roller in the lower left front of the machine; this is a friction roller, and it rotates the drum.

In the late 60's, Norge seems to have revised their basic design. (Figure NO-1) A V-belt was still used at the rear of the machine to drive a large fan behind the drum, but a multi-V-belt came off the front of the motor and went completely around the drum to rotate it.

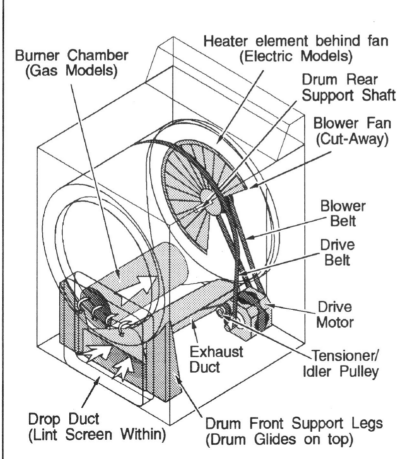

Figure NO-1: General Layout

Burner Chamber (Gas Models)

Heater element behind fan (Electric Models)

Drum Rear Support Shaft

Blower Fan (Cut-Away)

Blower Belt

Drive Belt

Drive Motor

Tensioner/ Idler Pulley

Exhaust Duct

Drop Duct (Lint Screen Within)

Drum Front Support Legs (Drum Glides on top)

The easiest way to tell the difference is that in early models, the rear panel of the cabinet is removable. In later models, the cabinet is solid on three sides; everything is accessed through the front. The very early model machines are quite difficult to get parts for, and if you can find them, they tend to be expensive. Considering the age of these machines, they are generally not worth fixing; thus, these machines are not covered in this book.

Most gas models have a burner located in the lower left side of the machine, accessible through an inspection plate in the front of the cabinet. In certain earlier models, the gas valve is located in the upper right side of the cabinet and is accessible through the door in the top of the cabinet. Electric models have a circular heater behind the drum and fan.

7-2 COMMON PROBLEMS

1) Since the drum is under pressure, rather than vacuum, a small amount of lint is always being blown through the felt drum seals. Thus, they tend to be very lint-y machines; wads of lint just seems to get around everywhere. These machines are also prone to lint build-up in the front drop-duct and exhaust. Symptoms are as described in Chapter 2. Open the duct as described in section 7-3 and clean out the lint.

2) A loud clattering sound as the machine is running usually means the blower hub is worn out. Remove the drum and replace the blower hub as described in section 7-4.

3) A scrubbing sound (metal-to-metal) usually means that the drum glides are worn out. Remove the drum as described in section 7-4 and replace the glides.

4) Heating problems. Diagnose and repair as described in Chapter 2.

5) Belt problems as described in Chapter 2. Replace and tension belts as described in section 7-4. Make sure you check the idler pulley for free movement.

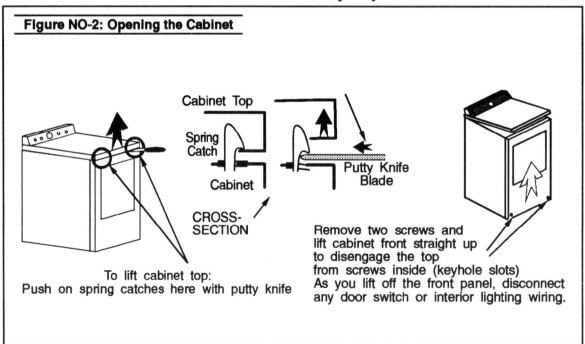

Figure NO-2: Opening the Cabinet

Cabinet Top

Spring Catch

Cabinet

CROSS-SECTION

Putty Knife Blade

To lift cabinet top:
Push on spring catches here with putty knife

Remove two screws and lift cabinet front straight up to disengage the top from screws inside (keyhole slots) As you lift off the front panel, disconnect any door switch or interior lighting wiring.

7-3 OPENING THE CABINET AND CLEANING OUT THE DUCTING

Opening the cabinet is pretty straightforward, as shown in figure NO-2. To clean out the drop duct remove the front panel. (Figure NO-3) To clean out the exhaust ducting remove the drum.

The multi-V drum drive belt may be replaced without removing the drum. Remove the front panel as shown in figure NO-2 . Cut out the old belt or lift the drum slightly and slip it past the drum glides, then slip the new one on. Install it around the tensioner as shown in figure NO-4.

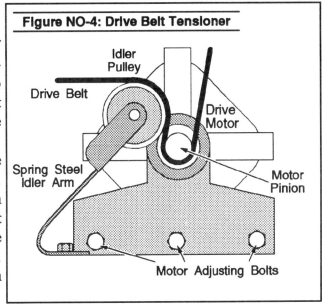

Figure NO-4: Drive Belt Tensioner

Idler Pulley
Drive Belt
Drive Motor
Spring Steel Idler Arm
Motor Pinion
Motor Adjusting Bolts

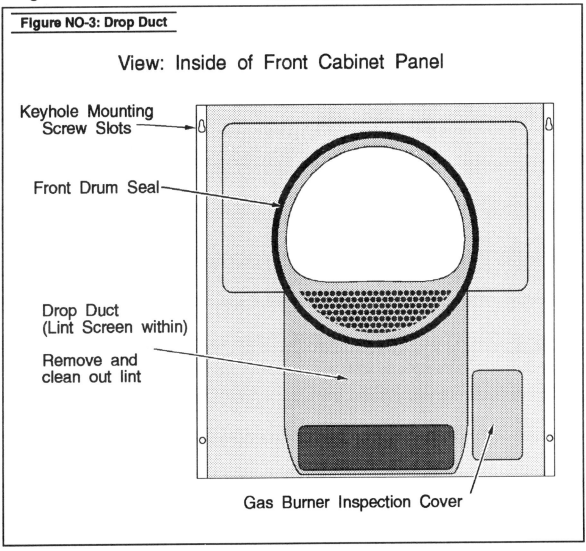

Figure NO-3: Drop Duct

View: Inside of Front Cabinet Panel

Keyhole Mounting Screw Slots

Front Drum Seal

Drop Duct (Lint Screen within)

Remove and clean out lint

Gas Burner Inspection Cover

7-4 DRUM REMOVAL

To replace the V-belt, blower hub, or electric heater element, you must remove the drum.

First, unplug the dryer and remove the front panel as described in section 7-3. Remove belt tension from the drive belt.

Inside the center rear of the drum there is a chrome plug. (Figure NO-5) Pop it off with a flat screwdriver. Inside you will see a bolt and washer; remove it. This bolt holds the drum and drum bearing to the drum shaft, so lift out the drum.

On the back side of the drum, in the center, you will see three bolts holding on the drum bearing housing. If you are going to replace the blower hub, replace the drum bearing, too.

To replace the blower hub, remove the washers from the drum shaft, carefully noting the order in which they come off. Remove the three bolts holding the fan to the hub. Release belt tension by working the belt off the motor pulley, then slip the hub and/or belt out of the hole and off the drum shaft.

In electric models, the heater element is located behind the heat shield plate behind the fan. Test the element for continuity and replace if defective. To access the element, remove the heat shield. If the heater is not pre-stretched, stretch it to approximately the correct length, but do not overstretch. It is better to leave it a little short, and work it to the correct length while in place. Don't forget to check the insulators and replace them if cracked or broken.

Re-assembly is basically the opposite of disassembly.

Fan belt tension was adjusted in two different ways. In some models, the motor is mounted in a pivoting motor mount whereby the weight of the motor keeps tension on the fan belt. In other models, fan belt tension is adjusted manually by loosening the three bolts at the base of the motor mounting plate (see figure NO-4) and pivoting the motor around the center bolt.

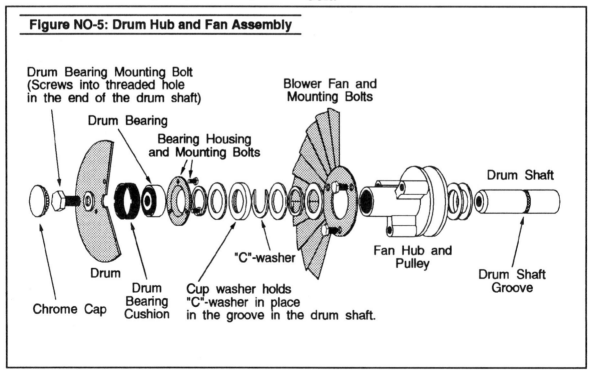

Figure NO-5: Drum Hub and Fan Assembly

Chapter 8

LATE MODEL MAYCOR
(Norge / Magic Chef / Admiral)

8-1 MACHINE LAYOUT

Figure NN-1 shows the general layout of these machines.

The rear of the drum is supported by two rollers. At the front, the drum is supported on the left side by a glide or roller mounted to a steel leg, which is welded to the baseplate. The front right side of the drum is supported by a glide which is molded into the blower housing.

The cabinet is solid on three sides, so everything is accessed through the front of the machine.

The blower fan is mounted directly to the front of the drive motor. The drive pulley and belt come off the rear of the motor, and the belt goes completely around the drum. The motor and blower are on the right side of the baseplate of the machine. A spring-loaded idler keeps tension on the belt.

In gas models the burner is on the left side of the baseplate of the machine. It is accessible through the small inspection door on the lower left front of the machine. In electric models, the heater is located at the top of the heat riser duct, at the left rear of the machine.

Operating thermostats in these machines are located on the front of the blower exhaust housing. Hi-limit stats are located on top of the heat riser duct.

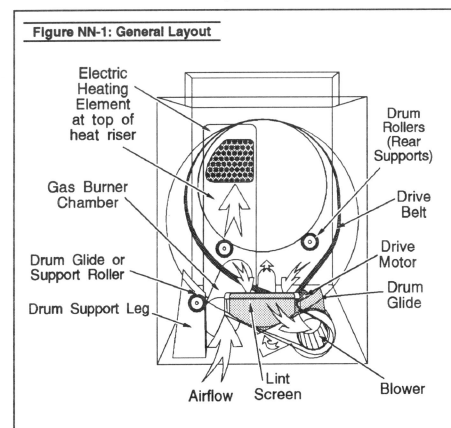

Figure NN-1: General Layout

Electric Heating Element at top of heat riser

Gas Burner Chamber

Drum Glide or Support Roller

Drum Support Leg

Airflow

Lint Screen

Drum Rollers (Rear Supports)

Drive Belt

Drive Motor

Drum Glide

Blower

8-2 COMMON PROBLEMS

The most common problems in these machines are as follows:

1) Loud rumbling or banging noise, getting progressively worse over time, or squeaky sounds coming from the drum support rollers. Also, scrubbing sounds (metal-to-metal) coming from worn drum glides. Remove the drum and replace the rollers or glides as described in section 8-3.

2) Heating problems. Diagnose and repair as described in chapter 2.

3) Drum doesn't turn, caused by a broken belt. You do not need to remove the drum to replace the belt in these machines. Replace as described in section 8-3.

4) No airflow, caused by the blower being clogged with lint. Remove the front panel and repair as described in section 8-3.

8-3 DISASSEMBLY

Lift the cabinet top by pushing on the spring clips as shown in figure NN-2.

With the top lifted, you have access to the electric heater element, located at the top left rear of the machine. Test as described in Chapter 2.

Remove the two screws inside the top of the cabinet front. Lift the front panel until the clips at the bottom of the panel disengage. Be careful to note the position of any door switch or other wiring and disconnect it as you remove the panel.

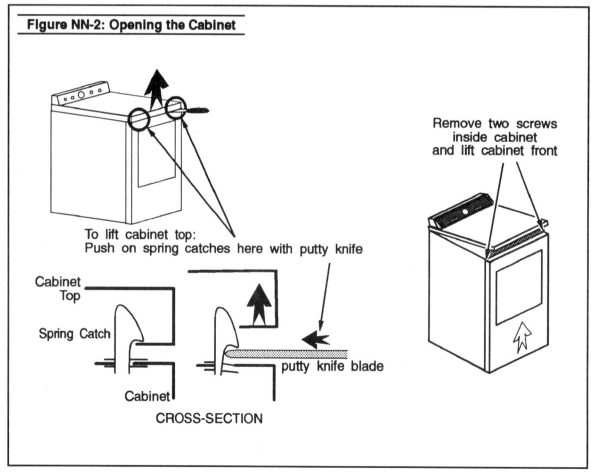

Figure NN-2: Opening the Cabinet

To lift cabinet top:
Push on spring catches here with putty knife

Cabinet Top

Spring Catch

Cabinet

putty knife blade

CROSS-SECTION

Remove two screws inside cabinet and lift cabinet front

With the front panel of the machine off, you can inspect or replace the belt. Reach between the blower housing and the drum and release tension, (figure NN-3) then lift the front end of the drum slightly to slip the belt between it and the front drum support. When installing the belt, make sure you get it into its groove in the drum.

BLOWER

To inspect, clean or replace the blower wheel, remove the blower inlet cover. The blower is held onto the motor shaft with a spring clip.

DRUM REMOVAL

With the cabinet top raised, the cabinet front removed and belt tension released, the drum just lifts out.

The drum support rollers are held to their shafts by a spring clip. (Figure NN-4) Check for free movement and wear and replace if bad.

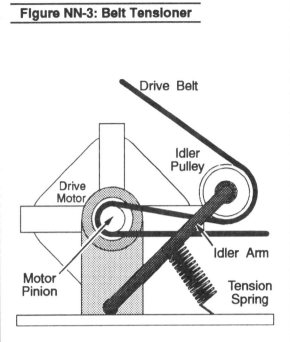

Figure NN-3: Belt Tensioner

Drive Belt

Idler Pulley

Drive Motor

Idler Arm

Motor Pinion

Tension Spring

Note: This is the view from the BACK side of the motor; as if you were standing on the INside of the dryer looking OUT!

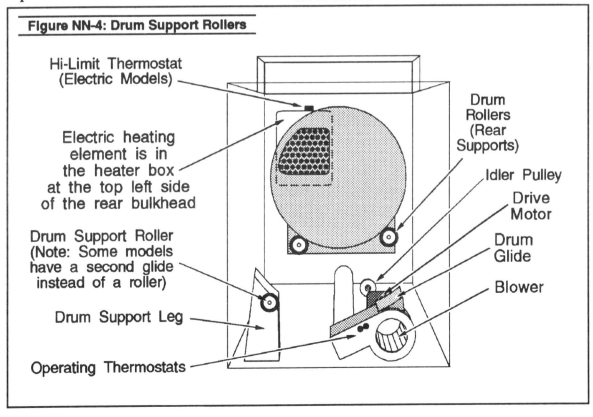

Figure NN-4: Drum Support Rollers

Hi-Limit Thermostat (Electric Models)

Electric heating element is in the heater box at the top left side of the rear bulkhead

Drum Support Roller (Note: Some models have a second glide instead of a roller)

Drum Support Leg

Operating Thermostats

Drum Rollers (Rear Supports)

Idler Pulley

Drive Motor

Drum Glide

Blower

The teflon friction surface of the drum support glide(s) can be easily removed and replaced. (Figure NN-5) Simply slip one end out of the slot and then slip the notched end off the pins that hold it in place.

The front and rear felt drum seals can also be inspected for wear at this point. They are glued in place. If you need to replace them, scrape them off and glue new ones on. When re-assembling the dryer, make sure these felt seals are not pinched or wrinkled.

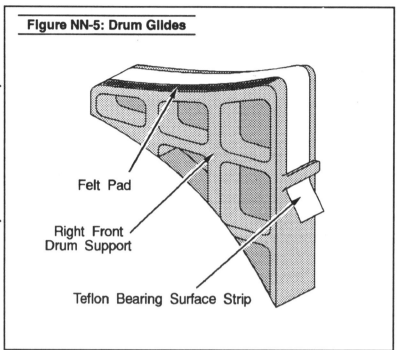

Figure NN-5: Drum Glides

Felt Pad

Right Front Drum Support

Teflon Bearing Surface Strip

Chapter 9

EARLY MODEL SPEED QUEEN

The easiest way to tell the difference between the early and late model Speed Queen machines is by the shape and location of the lint screen. In the early models, this screen is circular and fits into the door; in late models, the screen is in a slot below the door.

9-1 MACHINE LAYOUT

Figure S-1 shows the general layout of these machines.

The front of the drum in these machines is supported by two rollers. The rear of the drum is supported by a shaft at the rear of the machine.

The drive motor, located in the right rear of the machine, is belted directly to the drum. This belt comes off the *front* end of the motor; at the *back* end is another pulley and belt which drives a blower in the left rear of the machine. The blower takes suction through a tube which runs to a duct at the front of the machine.

In gas models, the burner assembly in these machines is located in the top right side of the machine. It is accessible through a door in the top of the cabinet.

The heater box in electric machines runs across the inside of the back of the machine near the top of the cabinet.

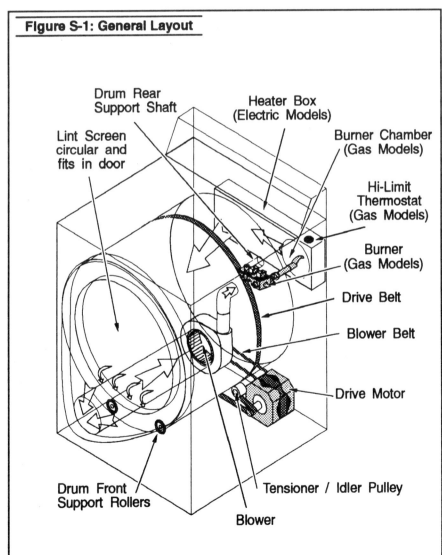

Figure S-1: General Layout

Drum Rear Support Shaft

Lint Screen circular and fits in door

Heater Box (Electric Models)

Burner Chamber (Gas Models)

Hi-Limit Thermostat (Gas Models)

Burner (Gas Models)

Drive Belt

Blower Belt

Drive Motor

Drum Front Support Rollers

Tensioner / Idler Pulley

Blower

9-2 COMMON PROBLEMS

The most common problems in these machines are:

1) Loud rumbling or banging noise, getting progressively worse over time. Caused by worn drum support rollers. Replace as described in section 9-4.

2) Heating problems. Diagnose and repair as described in chapter 2.

3) Squeaky sounds coming from the drum support rollers or the rear drum bearing. Replace as described in sections 9-3 or 9-4.

4) Drum doesn't turn, caused by a broken belt. Replace as described in section 9-3.

5) No airflow, caused by a broken blower belt or by seized bearings in the blower. Remove the back of the dryer and repair as described in section 9-3.

9-3 REAR CABINET ACCESS

To gain access to the blower, electric heater element, rear drum shaft bearings, or to remove the drive belt, first unplug the dryer. Remove the back cabinet panel by removing the screws holding it to the rest of the cabinet.

The electric heating element in these machines is located inside the heater box running across the top as you look in the back of the machine. (Figure S-2) Test as described in Chapter 2. If it's defective, disconnect the heater leads from the heater box terminals, remove the heater box and replace the element.

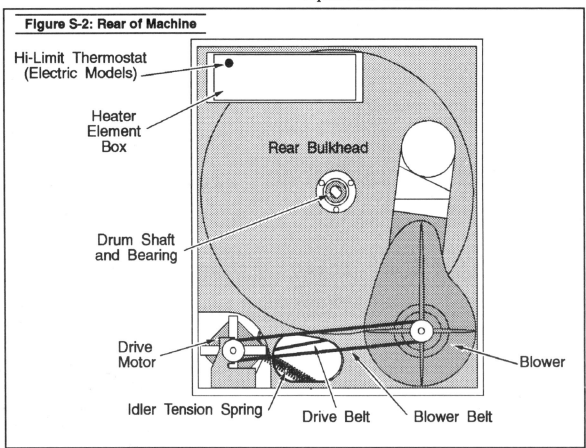

Figure S-2: Rear of Machine

Blower belt tension is adjusted by loosening the blower housing mounting screws and moving the blower housing. There is no tensioner. If you are not replacing the blower belt, simply run the belt off the pulley to remove.

Try turning the blower pulley by hand. If it is sticking or binding, the bearing must be replaced. Pull off the blower housing by removing the six screws that hold it in place.

NOTE: Do not try to press in a new bearing yourself. It is relatively easy to break the blower housing if it is not supported properly. Take your blower housing to a local appliance repair shop and have them do it.

To remove the drum shaft bearing or the drive belt, you must first remove drive belt tension. Just to the right of the drive motor you will see an inspection hole in the bulkhead. (Figure S-2) Inside the hole you can see the drive belt, tensioner, and spring. Unhook the spring from the baseplate and disengage the belt from the idler.

DRUM BEARING OR DRIVE BELT REPLACEMENT

Remove the center shaft bearing as shown in figure S-3. You will need circlip pliers to remove the circlip. When replacing the bearing, put one drop of oil on it but no more than that. Oil tends to attract dust; no good in a dryer. If you are replacing the drive belt, do not re-install the bearing yet.

Pull out any broken belt, or if you are replacing a worn belt, cut it and pull it out.

To put a new belt in, you must put it inside the rear bulkhead, around the drive shaft, then work it through the rear drum seal so it goes around the drum:

1) Take the twists out of the belt as much as possible, then work the belt inside the bulkhead through the drum shaft hole. Make sure the belt loops around the shaft.

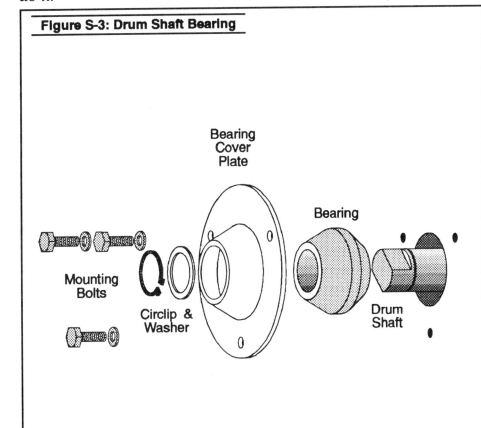

Figure S-3: Drum Shaft Bearing

Mounting Bolts

Circlip & Washer

Bearing Cover Plate

Bearing

Drum Shaft

2) Reach up inside the bulkhead, past the rear drum seal, and pull the belt down between the seal and the bulkhead. You should end up with one end of the belt sticking out the motor inspection hole and the other end looped around the shaft, visible through the drum shaft hole. (Figure S-4)

3) Push the belt up out of the way of the drum shaft hole and install the drum shaft bearing.

4) Using an open-end wrench on the flats of the drum shaft, turn the drum slowly *COUNTER-CLOCKWISE ONLY* and work the belt onto the outside of the drum. Try to keep the belt flat against the drum, with the grooves against the drum. (In other words, try to keep the belt from twisting too much as you install it.)

5) When you get the belt around the drum, turn the drum slowly and feel the rear drum seal with your fingers to make sure it's in place and not pinched. If you have a small inspection mirror, you can inspect it visually, too.

6) Run the belt around the motor pulley and tensioner as shown in figure S-5 and install the tension spring. Using your open-end wrench, continue turning the dryer drum slowly counterclockwise while guiding the belt into place on the drum with your other hand, until you're sure it won't pop off the pulley when you start the motor.

7) Don't forget to install and adjust the blower belt!

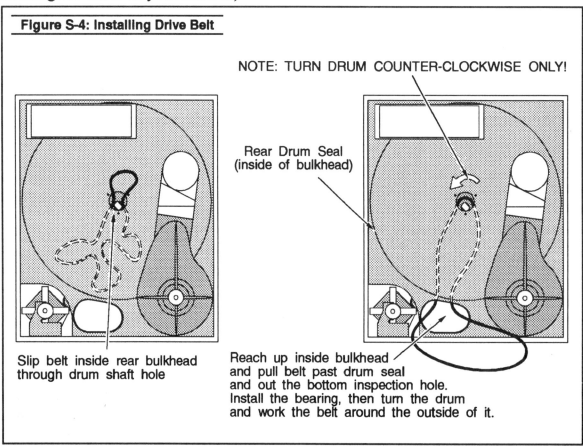

Figure S-4: Installing Drive Belt

NOTE: TURN DRUM COUNTER-CLOCKWISE ONLY!

Rear Drum Seal
(inside of bulkhead)

Slip belt inside rear bulkhead through drum shaft hole

Reach up inside bulkhead and pull belt past drum seal and out the bottom inspection hole. Install the bearing, then turn the drum and work the belt around the outside of it.

9-4 FRONT CABINET ACCESS

There are three ways to replace the drum support rollers, and all are difficult at best. The basic problem is that there is not enough clearance between the front bulkhead and the drum to get the rollers out once you've removed the mounting nuts.

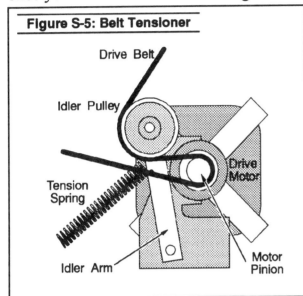

Figure S-5: Belt Tensioner

Drive Belt

Idler Pulley

Drive Motor

Tension Spring

Idler Arm

Motor Pinion

Figure S-6: Screws Under Door Seal

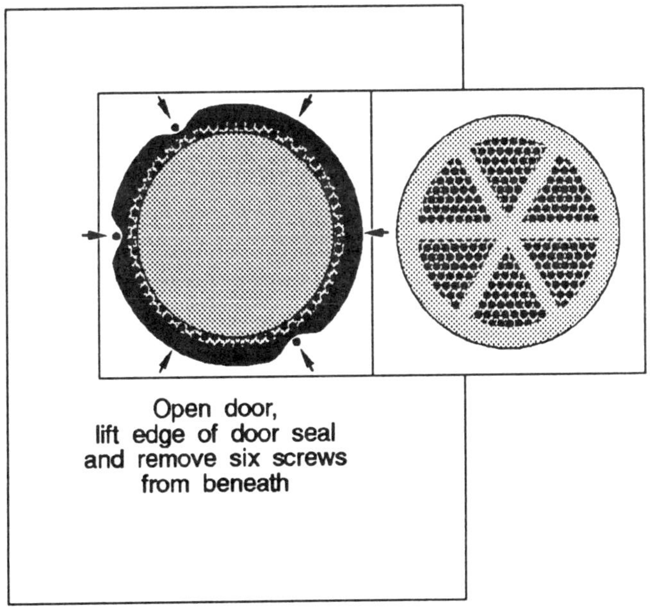

Open door, lift edge of door seal and remove six screws from beneath

The officially sanctioned way is to remove the dryer front panel, side panel, rear panel, and drum shaft and drum to get to the rollers. This is a long and involved process, even for professional technicians.

The method I recommend is that if you're really serious about keeping the dryer and getting it back into service, call a professional technician. It will be expensive, but these dryers are very very well-built and if the job is done right, you can probably expect a lot more service out of the thing.

A word of caution, however: decide up front what you're going to do, and follow through with it. Don't start working on it, and *then* decide it's too difficult and call a tech. Technicians *hate* it when customers do that. And you will be lucky to find an old-timer technician who will work on these old Speed Queen machines at all, much less if you have already started to dismantle it.

It is *possible* to change the rollers without removing the drum. I've heard of people doing it, but it's not recommended. The process involves using a crowbar to pry the drum and bulkhead apart slightly to get the rollers out. The danger, of course, is that you could bend the bulkhead or drum and ruin the dryer completely.

First, unplug the dryer. Remove the front of the cabinet; there are four screws at the base of the cabinet front, and six more around the clothes port. To see these six screws, you must lift the outer edge of the door seal. (Figure S-6) When you get all ten screws out, lift up on the bottom of the cabinet front panel until the top disengages from the cabinet.

In the lower right side of the front bulkhead, you will see an inspection hole. (Figure S-7) Reach into the inspection hole and feel the inside of the bulkhead, along the edge of the dryer drum. When you feel the drum support rollers, look outside the bulkhead in that same place and you will see the roller shaft nut. The second shaft nut (the left roller, as you look at the front of the machine) is located INSIDE the blower suction duct.

Remove these nuts to remove each roller. Remove only one roller at a time; it's easier to keep the drum supported. To prevent the shaft from turning with the nut, the inside end of the shaft has a flat screwdriver slot. If you drop the left nut down the duct, use a magnet to fish it out.

9-5 INSIDE THE CABINET TOP; BURNER SERVICE, THERMOSTAT LOCATION

To service the burner or the hi-limit stat on gas models, you must raise the top of the cabinet.

First, remove the front panel as described in section 9-4. Remove the two screws at the front corners of the cabinet top. Slide the cabinet top forward slightly to disengage the clips that hold down the back end of it, then lift it up.

THERMOSTAT LOCATIONS

The operating thermostats are located in the left front corner of the machine, on the blower suction duct in the front bulkhead. (Figure S-7) Remove the cabinet front to access. The hi-limit thermostat on electric models is fastened directly to the heater box. In gas models, the hi-limit stat is located inside the cabinet top, toward the right rear of the machine. Raise the cabinet top to access.

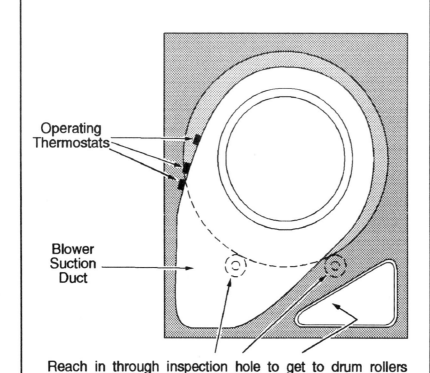

Figure S-7: Drum Roller Access

Operating Thermostats

Blower Suction Duct

Reach in through inspection hole to get to drum rollers

Mounting nut for left roller is inside of duct

Chapter 10

LATE MODEL SPEED QUEEN

The easiest way to tell the difference between the early and late model Speed Queen machines is by the shape and location of the lint screen. In the early models, this screen is circular and fits into the door; in late models, the screen is in a slot below the door.

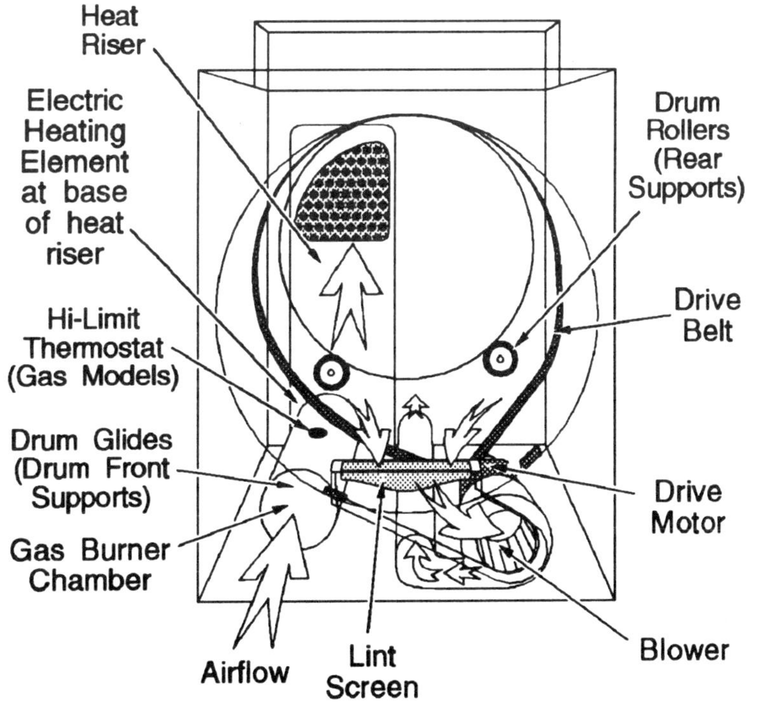

10-1 MACHINE LAYOUT

Figure SQ-1 shows the general layout of these machines.

The drum is supported at the front by two small glides beneath the drum. The rear of the drum is supported by rollers.

The cabinet is solid on three sides, so everything is accessed through the front of the machine.

The blower fan is mounted directly to the front of the drive motor. The drive pulley and belt come off the rear of the motor, and the belt goes completely around the drum. The motor and blower are on the right side of the baseplate of the machine. A spring-loaded idler, mounted to the motor baseplate, keeps tension on the belt.

In gas models the burner is on the left side of the baseplate of the machine. It is accessible through the small inspection door on the lower left front of the machine. In electric models, the heater is located at the bottom of the heat riser duct, at the left rear of the machine.

Figure SQ-1: General Layout

Heat Riser

Electric Heating Element at base of heat riser

Hi-Limit Thermostat (Gas Models)

Drum Glides (Drum Front Supports)

Gas Burner Chamber

Airflow

Lint Screen

Drum Rollers (Rear Supports)

Drive Belt

Drive Motor

Blower

Operating thermostats in these machines are located on the front of the blower exhaust housing. Hi-limit stats are located on top of the burner chamber in gas models, and directly on the heater panel in electric models.

10-2 COMMON PROBLEMS

The most common problems in these machines are as follows:

1) Rumbling or banging noise, getting progressively worse over time, or squeaky sounds coming from the drum support rollers. Replace the rollers as described in section 10-4.

2) Heating problems. Diagnose and repair as described in chapter 2.

3) Drum doesn't turn, caused by a broken belt. Replace as described in section 10-4.

4) No airflow, caused by the blower being clogged with lint. Remove the front panel and repair as described in section 10-3.

10-3 OPENING THE CABINET (Figure SQ-2)

Remove the two screws at the bottom of the cabinet front. Lift the bottom of the front panel until the clips at the top of the panel disengage from the top. Be careful to note the position of any door switch or other wiring and disconnect it as you remove the panel.

If you wish to lift the cabinet top, remove the two screws beneath the front corners.

BLOWER

To inspect, clean or replace the blower wheel, remove the blower inlet cover. The blower is threaded onto the motor shaft with a regular right-hand thread.

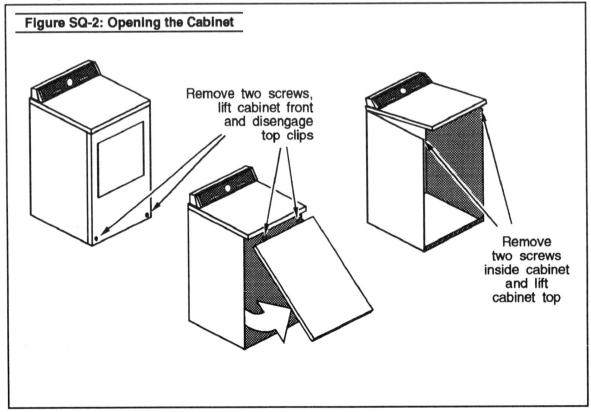

Figure SQ-2: Opening the Cabinet

Remove two screws, lift cabinet front and disengage top clips

Remove two screws inside cabinet and lift cabinet top

10-4 DRUM REMOVAL

To inspect and/or replace drum glides, belt or electric heater elements, you must remove the drum as follows:

1) Remove the cabinet front and the blower inlet duct as described in section 10-3.

2) Reach back and disengage the drive belt from the idler. (Figure SQ-3)

3) Remove the four screws from the front bulkhead as shown in figure SQ-4. Note that the bottom front corners of the bulkhead are supported by slots in the cabinet sides; this will help you support and align the bulkhead when assembling or disassembling. While holding the drum in place, lift out the bulkhead and set it aside. Then lift out the drum.

Figure SQ-3: Belt Tensioner

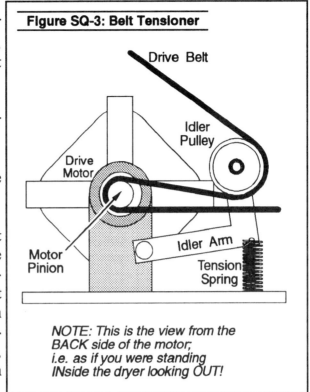

NOTE: This is the view from the BACK side of the motor; i.e. as if you were standing INside the dryer looking OUT!

Figure SQ-4: Front Bulkhead

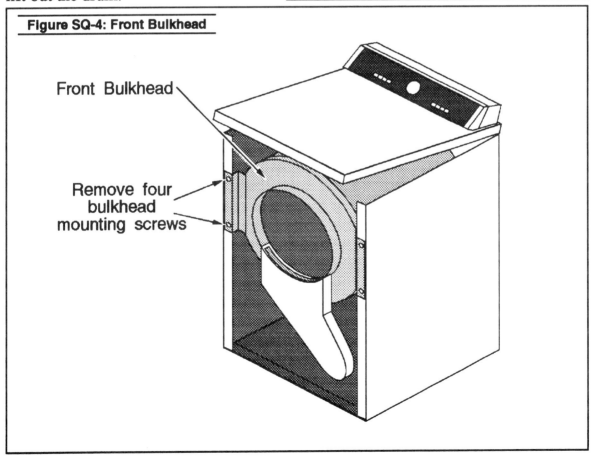

Front Bulkhead

Remove four bulkhead mounting screws

The drum glides are on the lower front corners of the inside of the bulkhead. Whether they're worn badly or not, replace them. They're cheap insurance against future problems.

The belt can be easily changed at this time. Don't forget to check the idler pulley for free movement.

The drum support roller shafts are held to the rear bulkhead by a nut. They have screwdriver slots cut into the top of the shaft for easy removal and replacement. (Figure SQ-5)

The front and rear felt drum seals can also be inspected for wear at this point. If you need to replace them, they are held on by a spring-loaded metal strap beneath them. Note that the outer edge of the front seal tucks beneath the lip on the front bulkhead. When re-assembling the dryer, make sure these felt seals are not pinched or wrinkled.

In electric models, the heater element is located inside the metal plate at the bottom of the heat riser at the left rear of the machine. Test it for continuity as described in Chapter 2 and replace if defective.

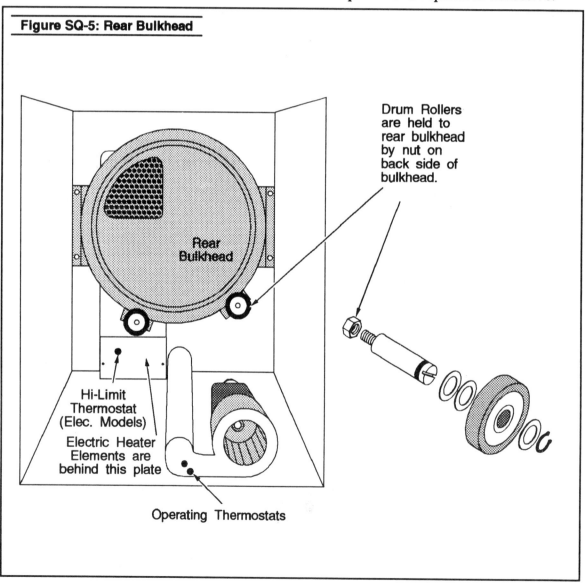

Figure SQ-5: Rear Bulkhead

Rear Bulkhead

Drum Rollers are held to rear bulkhead by nut on back side of bulkhead.

Hi-Limit Thermostat (Elec. Models)

Electric Heater Elements are behind this plate

Operating Thermostats

Chapter 11

WCI - WESTINGHOUSE

11-1 MACHINE LAYOUT

Figure WS-1 shows the general layout of these machines.

The front of the drum is supported by two small drum glides on top of the clothes port, which ride on the inside lip of the front of the drum. The rear of the drum is supported by a ball shaft in the center of the drum which rides in a plastic socket attached to the rear wall of the cabinet.

The blower fan is attached directly to the front of the drive motor. The drive belt comes directly off the rear of the motor and goes completely around the drum. The motor and blower are mounted on the right side of the baseplate of the machine. A spring-loaded idler pulley, mounted directly to the motor baseplate, keeps tension on the belt.

In gas models, the burner is mounted on the lower left side of the baseplate. It is accessible by removing the kickplate. The single circular heater element of electric models is located in a housing behind the drum.

The operating thermostats in these machines are located in just inside the door, on the right side of the door sill. The high-limit thermostats are mounted on the upper right side of the duct behind the drum. All thermostats can be accessed by removing the top panel of the cabinet as described in section 11-4.

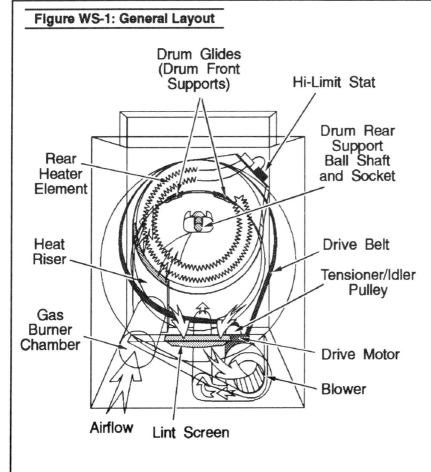

Figure WS-1: General Layout

Drum Glides (Drum Front Supports)

Hi-Limit Stat

Drum Rear Support Ball Shaft and Socket

Rear Heater Element

Heat Riser

Gas Burner Chamber

Drive Belt

Tensioner/Idler Pulley

Drive Motor

Blower

Airflow   Lint Screen

11-2 COMMON PROBLEMS

The most common problems in these machines are as follows:

1) Broken belts. The drum doesn't turn. Replace as described in section 11-4.

2) A loud growling noise, caused when the idler pulley seizes. Replace the idler arm as described in section 11-3.

3) Heating problems as described in Chapter 2. To access the gas burner, remove the kickplate as described in section 11-4. The heater element can be tested by lifting the cabinet top, but changing it requires drum removal.

4) A metal-to-metal scrubbing sound, caused when the front drum glides wear off. Remove the front of the machine as described in section 11-4, scrape off the old glides and felt seal and glue new ones on. A kit is available from your parts dealer.

5) Look at the circular center plate inside the rear of the dryer drum. (Figure WS-2) If the screws in the plate appear to be ripping it, you need to replace not only that plate, but also the rear drum ball shaft and bearing, as described in section 11-4.

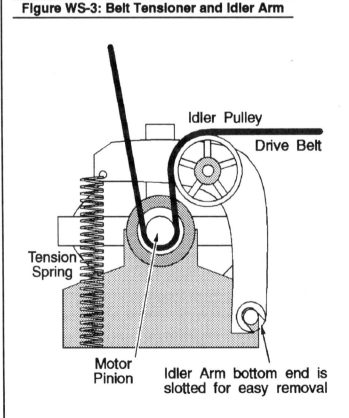

Figure WS-2: Centerplate

VIEW: Cut-Away through drum

Screws will tear through plate if there is too much friction in the rear drum support ball shaft and socket.

Figure WS-3: Belt Tensioner and Idler Arm

Idler Pulley

Drive Belt

Tension Spring

Motor Pinion

Idler Arm bottom end is slotted for easy removal

11-3 MOTOR, IDLER, AND BLOWER WHEEL

Looking at the rear of the machine, remove the inspection plate on the lower left corner. Inside this plate are the motor and idler. Slip the belt off the idler. The idler bracket is then easily removed as shown in figure WS-3.

If you need to service the motor or blower wheel, they are easily removed as a unit. Remove the two screws holding down the motor frame. The front end of the frame is attached by tabs that slip into the baseplate, so after removing the two screws, the motor and blower wheel will lift right out as an assembly. The blower cover is pressed against the blower housing by a spring between the cover and the motor.

In some models, the blower wheel is held to the motor shaft by a screw and a washer. In others, by a left hand thread; hold the motor shaft with a pair of vice grips and turn *clockwise* to remove it.

11-4 OPENING THE CABINET, BELT REPLACEMENT, DRUM REMOVAL

Remove the two screws at the bottom of the kickplate, then drop it down slightly to disengage the pins from the top.

If you are going to remove the drum, take tension off the belt as described in section 11-3.

If your machine has an enamelled top, raise the top of the cabinet by releasing the top corner clips as shown in figure WS-4. If you have a model with a galvanized cabinet top, remove the screws from the top panel and lift off the panel.

With the cabinet top raised, you can test the heater element for continuity. If it is bad, remove the drum as described below and replace it. If the new heater is not pre-stretched, stretch it to approximately the correct length, but do not overstretch. It is better to leave it a little short, and work it to the correct length while in place. Start from the middle of the element and work

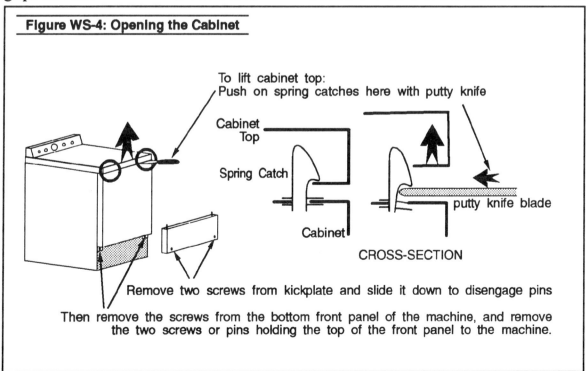

Figure WS-4: Opening the Cabinet

To lift cabinet top:
Push on spring catches here with putty knife

Cabinet Top

Spring Catch

Cabinet

putty knife blade

CROSS-SECTION

Remove two screws from kickplate and slide it down to disengage pins

Then remove the screws from the bottom front panel of the machine, and remove the two screws or pins holding the top of the front panel to the machine.

outward. And don't forget to check the insulators and replace them if cracked or broken.

Remove the one screw holding the blower suction duct to the blower housing. Then remove the two screws holding on the bottom of the cabinet front (four, on some models.) Next, remove the two screws at the top of the cabinet front panel. Disconnect the door switch as you lift the cabinet front off. Remember, as you remove the cabinet front, you are removing the drum front support, and the drum will be free-floating. If you are simply replac-ing the belt, slip the new belt around the drum and put the cabinet front right back on.

As soon as you have removed and set aside the cabinet front, lift the rear end of the drum and the ball shaft will disengage from its bearing socket. (Figure WS-5) With the drum out, you can now replace the ball shaft and bearing socket. A shaft and bearing kit is available from your parts dealer, including a special lithium grease used to lubricate the socket.

Reassembly is basically the opposite of disassembly.

Figure WS-5: Drum Removal

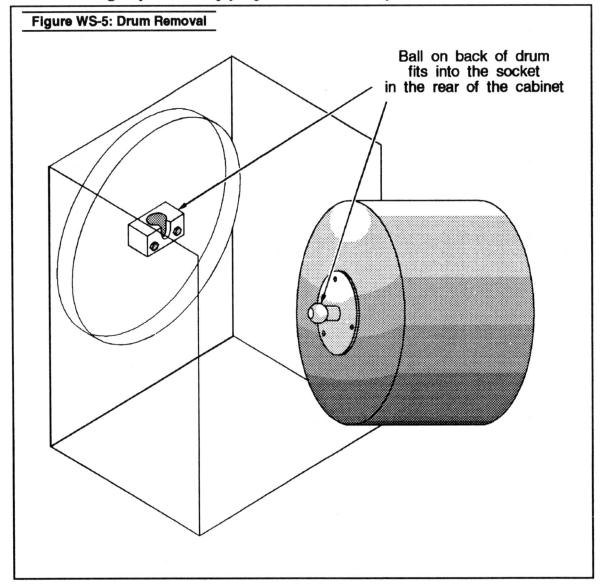

Ball on back of drum fits into the socket in the rear of the cabinet

Chapter 12

WCI - FRIGIDAIRE / FRANKLIN

There are two different designs, both related, covered in this chapter. There are minor differences in these designs, and one is almost a mirror image of the other. There are also differences in the individual components of the machines, so make sure you bring the model number with you when you go to your dealer for parts. But the way these machines are disassembled and serviced is essentially the same.

12-1 MACHINE LAYOUT (Figure F-1)

These two machines are known in the parts houses as the 5-roller Frigidaire and the 4-roller Frigidaire.

In both machines, the front of the drum is supported by two rollers. In 5-roller machines, the rear of the drum is supported by three rollers; in 4-roller machines, by two. These rollers are attached to the front and rear bulkheads.

In 5-roller machines, the gas burner chamber or electric heater box is circular and located on the left side of the baseplate. The motor and blower are located on the right side of the baseplate.

In 4-roller machines, the gas burner chamber or electric heater box are oval and located on the right side of the baseplate. The motor and blower are located on the left side of the baseplate.

In both machines, the rear bulkhead is also the air duct which channels air from the heater box or chamber into the drum. The front bulkhead likewise channels air from the drum into the blower suction.

The blower is attached directly to the front of the motor. The rear of the motor drives a belt which goes all the way around the drum. Belt tension is maintained by a spring-loaded idler pulley.

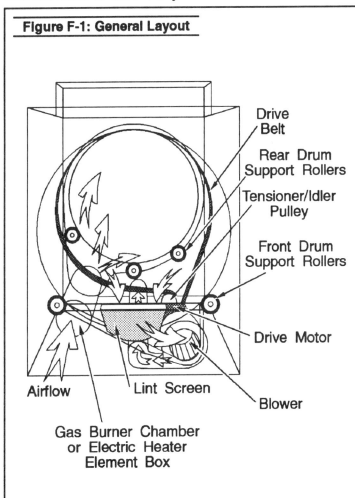

Figure F-1: General Layout

Drive Belt

Rear Drum Support Rollers

Tensioner/Idler Pulley

Front Drum Support Rollers

Drive Motor

Blower

Lint Screen

Airflow

Gas Burner Chamber or Electric Heater Element Box

12-2 COMMON PROBLEMS

1) Heating and airflow problems. These machines tend to get lint clogging the air holes in the front and rear bulkheads. This causes a number of different symptoms, mostly related to the airflow problems described in chapter 2. Since the rear bulkhead is welded in one piece, it can be difficult to clean out. Remove the drum as described in section 12-5 and clean out the air holes in the front and rear bulkheads as best you can.

2) A regular, loud, low-pitched banging sound generally means the rollers need to be replaced. Remove the drum as described in section 12-5 and replace the rollers.

3) If you hear a loud grinding noise, it may come from the blower wheel. Debris, such as pens and pencils and such, which are forgotten in the pockets of clothing, tends to get past the lint screen. They get into the blower wheel and absolutely waste it. Remove the motor as described in section 12-4 and inspect the blower wheel.

4) Heating problems as described in Chapter 2.

12-3 HEATER AND GAS BURNER ACCESS

Remove the bottom front panel of the cabinet as shown in figure F-2.

Beneath the panel there is an access hole in the cabinet front. Through this hole, you can get to the gas burner or electric heater box for testing and repair as described in Chapter 2. If the electric heater element is bad, replace the whole heater box. The element alone *can* be replaced, but it is a real bear of a job.

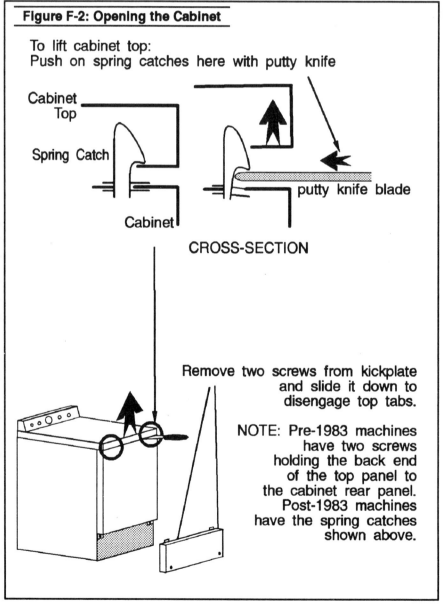

Figure F-2: Opening the Cabinet

To lift cabinet top:
Push on spring catches here with putty knife

Cabinet Top

Spring Catch

Cabinet

putty knife blade

CROSS-SECTION

Remove two screws from kickplate and slide it down to disengage top tabs.

NOTE: Pre-1983 machines have two screws holding the back end of the top panel to the cabinet rear panel. Post-1983 machines have the spring catches shown above.

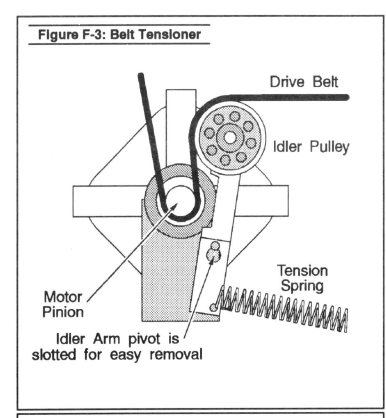

Figure F-3: Belt Tensioner

Drive Belt

Idler Pulley

Tension Spring

Motor Pinion

Idler Arm pivot is slotted for easy removal

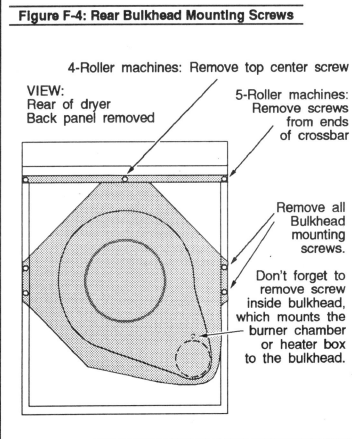

Figure F-4: Rear Bulkhead Mounting Screws

4-Roller machines: Remove top center screw

VIEW:
Rear of dryer
Back panel removed

5-Roller machines:
Remove screws
from ends
of crossbar

Remove all
Bulkhead
mounting
screws.

Don't forget to
remove screw
inside bulkhead,
which mounts the
burner chamber
or heater box
to the bulkhead.

The gas burner and heater box are also removable through this hole; you do not need to remove the drum. However, in electric models, you do need to remove the rear panel of the dryer, in order to get to the screw holding the heater box to the rear bulkhead.

12-4 BELT REPLACEMENT AND ACCESS TO BLOWER AND IDLER

Remove the rear panel from the cabinet. Inside, you will see the motor and idler. (Figure F-3) Remove the belt from the idler. The idler arm pivot hole is elongated, so if you need to replace the idler pulley, simply lift the whole idler arm off its pivot stud.

Reach inside the bulkhead and remove the screw holding the heater box or burner chamber to the rear bulkhead.

To replace the belt, you do not need to remove the rear bulkhead. Just remove the bulkhead mounting screws (figure F-4) two at a time. As you remove each pair, slip the belt over the bulkhead and replace the screws. Don't forget to work the belt past the heater box inside, too.

Work the belt into place and around the idler as shown in figure F-3. Turn the drum several times to make sure the belt won't jump the motor pulley. Also start the machine with the rear panel off and observe the belt for proper operation.

Inspecting or servicing the blower does not require pulling the rear bulkhead, either. First, take the belt off the idler and disconnect the motor wiring harness. Remove the bolt holding the motor mounting plate to the dryer baseplate, and the two screws holding the motor mounting plate to the front bulkhead. (Figure F-5) There is also a tab at the front end of the motor mounting plate which slides into a slot in the baseplate, so slide the motor towards the rear of the dryer to disengage this tab. Then lift out the motor and blower assembly. The blower cover in these machines is held against the blower housing by a spring around the motor shaft, so it just pops off.

Some models have a clamp holding the blower wheel to the motor shaft. Others have a solid metal cap with a little barb in it. These are just about impossible to remove without breaking the blower wheel; if you remove the blower wheel, plan on replacing it.

Assembly is the opposite of disassembly. Make sure you check the blower cover gasket for wear and the idler pulley for free movement.

12-5 DRUM REMOVAL

To replace the drum support rollers, drum felt seals, or to clean out the front or rear bulkhead air ducts, you must remove the drum.

Remove the rear cabinet panel and release belt tension as described in section 12-4. Reach inside the rear bulkhead and remove the screw holding the heater box or burner chamber to the bulkhead. Press your knees against the rear bulkhead and remove the four screws holding the sides of the bulkhead to the cabinet. (Figure F-4) Keeping your knees against the rear bulkhead, remove the two screws holding the top crossbar to the cabinet. The weight of the drum and rear bulkhead is now on the top crossbar and your knees. Remove the rear bulkhead and drum.

Check the air holes in the front and rear bulkheads for lint clogging. There is no fast, easy way to clean them out. It's a tedious, hole-by-hole process.

Also while you're in there, you might want to replace the rollers, whether they're making noise or not. It's cheap insurance against future problems. They are held to their shafts by circlips. Put just a little bit of grease on each roller, but not much. Oil and grease tend to attract dust and lint.

The felt seals are glued to the front and rear bulkheads. To replace, scrape them off and clean the surface thoroughly with some rubbing alcohol. Then glue new ones on.

Assembly is the opposite of disassembly. Check that the rollers are against the bulkheads with the drum in place.

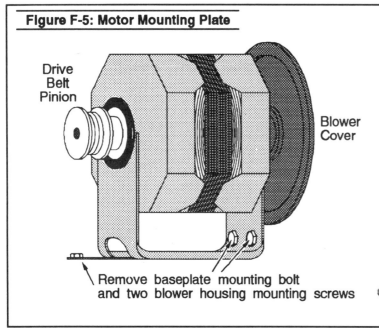

Figure F-5: Motor Mounting Plate

Drive Belt Pinion

Blower Cover

Remove baseplate mounting bolt and two blower housing mounting screws

ROLLER ADJUSTMENT

The center rear roller should bear almost none of the weight of the drum when it's empty; it only bears part of the load when there are clothes in the dryer. It should be turning when the drum is empty and turning, but it should stop with light pressure from your fingers. Loosen the screws mounting it to the rear bulkhead and adjust it accordingly.

12-6 THERMOSTATS

The thermostats in these machines are located in the usual places; the hi-limit stat is on top of the burner chamber or heater box, and the operating thermostats are on the blower outlet. All are accessible through the bottom front inspection panel.

For some strange reason in some models, Frigidaire decided that they didn't want to use two or three operating thermo-stats like everyone else. Frigidaire engineers actually wrapped them into one, giving us three-, four- and even five-lead thermostats. (Figure F-6) Some thermostats have internal bias heaters, some external bias heaters. The function of these bias heaters is to generate some heat WITHIN the thermostat itself, which will make the thermostat open sooner, which will make the dryer operate at a lower temperature.

These special thermostats are about three to five times more expensive than regular two-lead stats, and they are not easy to test. Replace if you suspect they're defective. Four and five-lead thermostats are double-throw thermostats with a bias heater. (See Chapter 2, section 2-4(c) about 3-lead thermostats) Thus, a timer advancement problem in the automatic cycle may be traceable to a 4- or 5-lead stat.

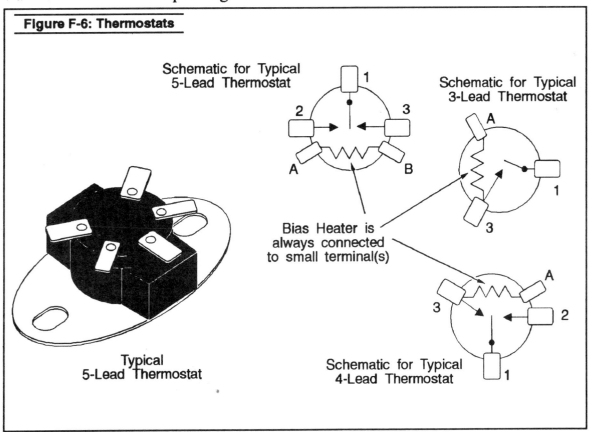

Figure F-6: Thermostats

Schematic for Typical 5-Lead Thermostat

Schematic for Typical 3-Lead Thermostat

Bias Heater is always connected to small terminal(s)

Typical 5-Lead Thermostat

Schematic for Typical 4-Lead Thermostat

Index

ABOUT THE AUTHOR

Douglas Emley is Chief Officer in charge of hazardous materials on-board a Merchant Marine ship. He holds a Bachelor of Science degree, engineer's license and officer's license from the Kings Point Merchant Marine Academy, Long Island, New York. Emley has been a major appliance service technician for nearly ten years. Tired of seeing individuals pay his service fees for simple repairs, Emley decided to write easy-to-understand repair guides. "The manufacturers service manuals are too confusing for the average do-it-yourselfer. In my opinion, they contain far too much unnecessary information."

To simplify the diagnosis and repair process, Emley deliberately avoids technical terminology in his instructions. "I'd rather show the average person how to save a fortune by diagnosing the problem themselves and fixing the simple stuff -- 95% of all repairs! When there's a *serious* problem, then call out the tech and pay for his expertise."

If you found this guide easy-to-follow and helpful, you may be interested in Emley's other repair guides:

The No Headache Guide to Home Repair Series--
Washing Machine Repair Under $40 -- ISBN 1-884348-02-5
Refrigerator Repair Under $40 -- ISBN 1-884348-00-9
Dishwasher Repair Under $40 -- ISBN 1-884348-03-3

These books can be ordered through your local library, bookstore or by mail order. Send check or money order to: New Century Publishing, P.O. Box 9861, Fountain Valley, CA 92708. Each title is $12.95; please include $2.50 shipping via book rate (allow 4 to 5 weeks delivery) or $4.50 shipping via Air Mail. California residents please add 7.75% sales tax. Volume discounts are available by calling (714)554-2020.